Thank God!! :)
We're debt free!!
$83,900 in
20 months
  - Jesse + Jenn

Michelle Sinkovitz,
35K in 15 months!
Thank you so much
Dave! You are really
an inspiration to
so many!

107 in 1001
days! We're
debt free!!
Erin & Kevin
Phoenix AZ

$51,000 PAID OFF
AT 51 YEARS OLD!
I am debt free!
Elaine Davila

Kyle + Amber White
$36,000 in 7 months!
Say NO to debt!!

WE'RE DEBT FREE!!
THANKS FOR EVERYTHING
DAVE!
  Mike & Cathy

To God Be The Glory!
We're Debt FREE!!!
The Schmersal Family!
$120,000.00 Paid off 34 mths.
William Luke Faith Rob♡Anji
  Rebekah Lydia

Debt free!
  - Jen + Tim

Dave and Kim Monk (Troy, IL)
$137,000 in 3½ years!
* including our home! :)
☑ Baby step 6

We're debt free!
119,500/35 mo
We did it, so can you
Stephanie & David

THIS BOOK BELONGS TO

START DATE
THE DAY YOU DECIDED TO CHANGE

_____ / _____ / _____
MONTH   DAY   YEAR

WE ALL MESS UP

We've all done stupid. I did stupid with zeros on the end.

I started from nothing. But by the time I was 26, I had a net worth of a little over a million dollars. And then it all came crashing down.

The short story? I had a lot of debt. And it caused me to lose everything. That was the bottom for me.

You might be on your way to the bottom. You might already be there. Or maybe you were the smart one who didn't borrow money at all. No matter where you are, you can always do better.

And you're not alone.

I discovered God's and Grandma's ways of handling money and learned that the only way to change my situation was to change the guy in my mirror. So, I changed. It was a long, painful process, but it worked. And it will work for you too.

For three decades, nearly 10 million people have found success with the same proven plan that you're about to follow. Stick with us, stay focused, and follow each step, and I promise, you *will* change your life.

If you'll live like no one else now, later you can live and give like no one else.

You got this! It's game on.

THE 7 BABY STEPS

OUR *Proven* PLAN

If you want to win with money, you can't do what you've always done. You need a plan that works. That's why Dave created the 7 Baby Steps. It's a clear path to know where you are and where you're headed next. This isn't a get-rich-quick scheme, and you haven't won the lottery. But if you follow each step—in order and with great focus and intentionality—you will change your life.

1 BABY STEP 1
Save $1,000 for Your Starter Emergency Fund

2 BABY STEP 2
Pay Off All Debt (Except the House) Using the Debt Snowball

3 BABY STEP 3
Save 3–6 Months of Expenses in a Fully Funded Emergency Fund

4 BABY STEP 4
Invest 15% of Your Household Income in Retirement

5 BABY STEP 5
Save for Your Children's College Fund

6 BABY STEP 6
Pay Off Your Home Early

7 BABY STEP 7
Build Wealth and Give

COURSE OVERVIEW

You've learned the Baby Steps, but that's not the whole course! You've got nine video lessons ahead of you. The first four will walk you through our proven plan, the 7 Baby Steps. And the last five lessons will teach you how to tackle life on the plan. Let's break it down.

BABY STEPS 4 5 6 7
Page 58

BABY STEP 3
Page 44

BABY STEP 2
Page 28

BABY STEP 1 **&BUDGETING**
Page 12

LESSON 04

LESSON 03

LESSON 02

LESSON 01

THE plan

Lessons 1–4 walk you through the 7 Baby Steps. This is your proven plan to win with money. In these lessons, you'll learn how to do more than just treat the symptoms of your money problem. You'll get to the root of the problem: your behavior!

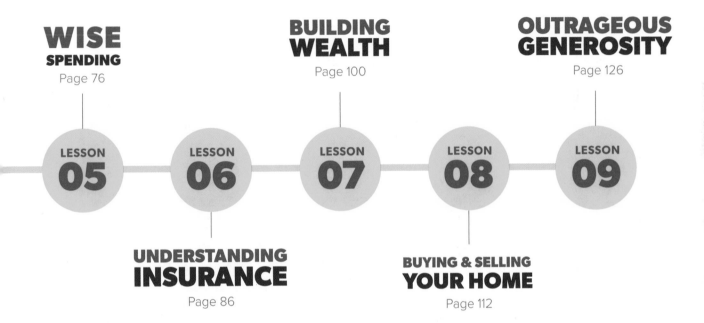

WISE
SPENDING
Page 76

BUILDING
WEALTH
Page 100

OUTRAGEOUS
GENEROSITY
Page 126

LESSON
05

LESSON
06

LESSON
07

LESSON
08

LESSON
09

UNDERSTANDING
INSURANCE
Page 86

BUYING & SELLING
YOUR HOME
Page 112

Lessons 5–9 keep you on track with the Baby Steps. Learn to navigate spending, insurance, real estate and investing so you don't ruin your progress! And protect yourself and your money so you can start fighting for the things you want.

MEET THE *Team*

Whether you've done stupid with zeros on the end or you're just trying to do a little better, we know that money is a big deal in your life. You may feel ashamed. You may feel stressed. Or you might be a little unsure of what to do with your money.

That's why we have a team who's been where you are right now. They know how to win with money, and they'll help you get there too.

Dave Ramsey, Rachel Cruze, George Kamel and Dr. John Delony are all Ramsey Personalities and America's trusted authorities on the most important areas of your life, including money! Their #1 bestselling books, podcasts and shows have helped change the lives of millions of people. And starting today, they're going to help you change yours.

Dave RAMSEY

After battling his way out of bankruptcy and millions of dollars in debt, Dave Ramsey started on a mission to make sure other people discovered the way out. That's why he created *Financial Peace University*. Today, nearly 10 million people have experienced life-change through this course. And he's helped millions more as a #1 national bestselling author, personal finance expert and host of *The Ramsey Show*, heard by more than 18 million listeners each week. He's authored eight national bestselling books, including *The Total Money Makeover*, *EntreLeadership*, and his latest, *Baby Steps Millionaires*. He also serves as CEO for Ramsey Solutions. Since 1992, Dave has helped people regain control of their money, build wealth, and enhance their lives. His biblical, commonsense advice is for anyone ready to win with money.

> **Live like no one else so later you can live and GIVE** *like no one else."*

John DELONY

Dr. John Delony is a national bestselling author, mental health and wellness expert, host of *The Dr. John Delony Show* and co-host of *The Ramsey Show*. He holds two PhDs—one in counseling and the other in higher education. Before joining Ramsey Solutions, John spent nearly two decades working as a senior leader at multiple universities, a professor and researcher, and a crisis responder. Now, as a Ramsey Personality, he teaches people how to reclaim their lives from the madness of the modern world. He's authored two books, including his latest, *Own Your Past, Change Your Future: A Not-So-Complicated Approach to Relationships, Mental Health, and Wellness*. John's goal is to help you navigate tough decisions, improve your relationships, and believe you're worthy of being well.

> **FRIENDS are your emergency fund *for life.***

Rachel CRUZE

Rachel Cruze grew up learning how to win with money. As Dave Ramsey's daughter, she's seen the dangers of debt firsthand and understands the power of budgeting. But, as she'll tell you, she's a natural spender and hated budgeting until she discovered what a budget can really do!

Rachel is a #1 *New York Times* bestselling author, financial expert, host of *The Rachel Cruze Show* and co-host of *The Ramsey Show*. She's the author of three bestselling books, including her latest, *Know Yourself, Know Your Money: Discover WHY You Handle Money the Way You Do, and WHAT to Do About It!* Since 2010, Rachel has served at Ramsey Solutions, where she teaches people how to avoid debt, save money, budget and win with money at any stage of life. And she does it all with a dose of fun! Rachel is an energetic and thought-provoking speaker who travels the country teaching thousands of people how to live a life they love.

> **A budget doesn't LIMIT your freedom. A budget *gives you freedom.*"**

George *KAMEL*

George Kamel is a personal finance expert with a countercultural approach to money. Since 2013, George has served at Ramsey Solutions and has faithfully walked the Baby Steps—climbing from $40,000 in consumer debt to Baby Step 7 in eight years. Today, as a Ramsey Personality, George is the host of *The Fine Print*, a co-host of *The Ramsey Show*, a speaker and the friend who has your back. His mission is to help people spend less, save more, avoid consumer traps, and have some good laughs along the way.

> **If you follow the TRENDS, you will fall for *the traps.*"**

A budget gives you **PERMISSION** to spend.

— RACHEL CRUZE

LESSON 1

BABY STEP 1 & BUDGETING

KEY POINTS

- The 7 Baby Steps focus on changing your behavior toward money through a proven, step-by-step plan.

- Baby Step 1 is saving $1,000 for your starter emergency fund.

- A zero-based budget is the tool that helps you take control of your money.

BABY STEP

1

Save $1,000 for Your Starter Emergency Fund

Your first goal is to save $1,000 for your starter emergency fund as fast as you possibly can. You have to make saving a priority. Focus all of your energy on getting this Baby Step done—fast! An emergency is going to happen, so you have to be ready when it hits. We're talking no credit cards, but real cash in the bank to cover it.

GUIDE
Dave Ramsey

GUIDE
Rachel Cruze

BABY STEP 1

Save ___1,000___ for your starter emergency fund.

If you will live like no one else now, later you can live and ___Give___ like no one else.

No *discipline* seems pleasant at the time, but painful. Later on, however, it produces a *harvest* of righteousness and peace for those who have been trained by it.

— **HEBREWS 12:11** (NIV)

BUDGETING

A budget is simply a ___Plan___ for your money.

A zero-based budget means that your income minus your expenses equals ___zero___.

The ___Free Spirit___ feels controlled by the budget.

The ___Nerd___ enjoys doing the budget.

LESSON 1 //
BUDGETING

In the Budget Committee _____, you'll meet with your spouse to review next month's budget.

The budget gives you _____ you never knew you had.

> **Suppose one of you wants to build a tower. Won't you first sit down and estimate the** *cost* **to see if you have enough money to** *complete* **it?**
>
> — **LUKE 14:28** (NIV)

NOTES

_____

_____

_____

_____

_____

_____

_____

_____

ANSWER KEY

Meeting
Control

LESSON 1 //
BUDGETING

BUDGET WITH EVERYDOLLAR

Ready to take control of your money and start making progress toward your Baby Step goal? In the Action Steps, you'll create your own zero-based budget with the premium version of EveryDollar! Great news—you get this free as part of your Ramsey+ membership!

You'll have a One-Minute Takeaway at the end of every lesson! Wait here until the video ends.

One-Minute
TAKEAWAY

NERD & *Free Spirit* QUIZ

Pic 2020

Post covi Soil turmoil

PERSON 1

A B

PICK THE ONE THAT SOUNDS MOST LIKE YOU

PERSON 2

A B

A: You're prepared for Tax Day months in advance.
B: Tax Day? That's in October, right?

A: Rules are important and should always be followed.
B: Rules are more like suggestions.

A: You are always on time. Always.
B: You show up "on time," give or take 15 minutes.

A: You make a plan for each day of your vacation.
B: Vacations are more fun with no schedule.

A: You read the introductions of books.
They're in there for a reason!
B: You skip introductions—only chapters count.

A: Your life's motto: "A place for everything
and everything in its place."
B: You live by the phrase, "It'll all work out!"

A: You organize your shirts by color. Doesn't everyone?
B: You're doing good just to get your shirts off the floor.

A: You can't wait to create your EveryDollar budget!
*B: You're considering faking an illness for the
Budget Committee Meeting.*

**TOTAL YOUR SCORES AND
CIRCLE THE HIGHEST ONE**

Person 1: A: 4 B: 4

Person 2: A: 1 B: 8

IF YOU HAD A HIGH SCORE OF: A

SCORE

4–5: NERD-ISH
You have a pretty good idea of how much money is in your account.

6–7: NERD
Budgets are for awesome people.

8: ULTRA NERD
You canceled your plans with friends so you could start drafting next month's budget.

IF YOU HAD A HIGH SCORE OF: B

SCORE

4–5: FREE SPIRIT-ISH
You've got a budget somewhere. You could find it if you needed to.

6–7: FREE SPIRIT
Budgets are for boring people.

8: ULTRA FREE SPIRIT
Budgets are like putting on a straitjacket. Why would you ever do that to yourself?

OFFICIAL RULES OF THE
BUDGET COMMITTEE
MEETING

FOR THE NERD

1. Create the budget.
2. Thank the Free Spirit for being there!
3. Show the budget to the Free Spirit. Then be quiet.

FOR THE FREE SPIRIT

1. Come to the Budget Committee Meeting.
2. Be realistic and don't use the phrase "whatever you want."
3. Have an opinion and change something.

WHAT TO DO:

Fill out your estimated monthly expenses for the following categories. Then add up the total for all categories.

SEE WHAT YOU'RE *Spending*

Now that you know whether you're more of a Nerd or a Free Spirit, it's time to take the first step into budgeting. Don't panic—this first step is simple!

THE BUDGET IS YOUR MAP FOR THE MONTH

Rachel taught you how to create a zero-based budget with EveryDollar. But to get to where you want to go, you have to know where you are.

It's just like driving: If you don't know your starting point, it's impossible to get to your destination! That's why you do a **Quick-Start Budget.**

IT'S TIME TO FILL OUT THE QUICK-START BUDGET

This activity is a simple way to put pen to paper and get you thinking about how much you're currently spending in each category, each month. You'll notice there are a few categories missing, like income and debt. That's okay! Remember, this is just your starting point.

Free Spirits, make sure there's fun in the budget!

Nerds, this is where you get to work with numbers!

☐ **STEP 1**

Write down what you're spending for the month in each item of each category. If you don't know exact numbers, just make your best guess!

☐ **STEP 2**

Add up each item in each category and write the TOTAL at the bottom.

☐ **STEP 3**

Add up the numbers in all of the TOTAL boxes and write that number in the TOTAL FOR ALL CATEGORIES box.

YOUR QUICK-START BUDGET

Follow Steps 1–3 on the previous page to list and add up your monthly expenses.

♥ GIVING — Planned

Church	$
Charity	$
TOTAL	$

🍴 FOOD — Planned

Groceries	$ 400
Restaurants	$ 0
TOTAL	$ 0

👕 PERSONAL — Planned

Clothing	$
Phone	$ 70
Fun Money	$
Gifts	$
TOTAL	$ 70

🚙 TRANSPORTATION — Planned

Auto Insurance	$
Gas	$
Maintenance	$
TOTAL	$

🏠 HOUSING — Planned

Mortgage/Rent	$ 1200
Utilities	$ 260
TOTAL	$ 1460

Debt =

TOTAL FOR ALL CATEGORIES $ 1870

w/ out Debt

Remember, this total does not include every category that will be in your monthly budget—just a few of the big ones!

1800

Great Start!

You've taken the first step to creating your monthly budget. In the Action Steps, you'll **create a zero-based budget with EveryDollar—just like Rachel showed you!**

DISCUSSION

This is where change happens—in a safe space where you can talk about real life. This is where you *start* connecting with other people and *stop* believing you're in this alone. Whether you're taking this class online or in person, be honest with your answers and remember to encourage one another!

 Think about a time when an emergency stressed you out. How would a starter emergency fund have made that a *stress-free* emergency?

 What are some categories that you think might bust your budget? What can you do to keep those categories under control?

 Cashing out your budget can help you stay ahead of problem categories. Which categories could you use cash for to help you stick to your budget?

 Based on your results from the Nerd & Free Spirit Quiz, what strengths can you bring to the Budget Committee Meeting?

ACTION STEPS

Personal finance is 80% behavior. It's only 20% head knowledge.
So, it's time to live out what you just learned! Complete each of the
Action Steps before the next lesson. (If you're married, do this with
your spouse.) You got this!

☐ **SET UP YOUR RAMSEY+ MEMBERSHIP**
Your **Ramsey+ membership** is the one-stop shop for
everything you need to win with money—tools, education,
custom recommendations, financial coaching and more!
Be sure to answer every question that pops up in your
membership—your answers help us personalize your plan and
give you a great picture of where you stand today.

☐ **CREATE A BUDGET WITH EVERYDOLLAR**
Your Quick-Start Budget was a great way to get
the hang of budgeting. Now you'll create a zero-
based budget with **EveryDollar.** Married couples, don't
forget the Budget Committee Meeting. And singles, show
your budget to your accountability partner. If you need extra
guidance, watch the budgeting videos in your membership!

☐ **SAVE MONEY IN BABY STEP 1**
It's time to draw a line in the sand! If you're on Baby Step 1,
see how much money you can save in just one week and then
track your savings progress in **Ramsey+**. If you've already got
your $1,000, well done! Move on to the next Action Step.

☐ **COMPLETE YOUR FINANCIAL SNAPSHOT**
If you're in a class, fill out the Financial Snapshot card found
in this lesson and turn it in to your coordinator at the start of
Lesson 2.

☐ **READ "THE POWERFUL ZERO-BASED BUDGET" ON
THE NEXT PAGE**
Want a quick refresher on how to easily make a zero-based
budget with **EveryDollar**? Read on!

THE *Powerful* ZERO-BASED BUDGET

Whether you're on Baby Step 1 or 7, you need a budget. It's your map for every month. And it puts you in control of your money.

Want to pay off debt? *You need a budget.* Want to build your emergency fund? *You need a budget.* Already investing? You're not off the hook—*you still need a budget.* And not just any budget—that's right, a zero-based budget.

A zero-based budget simply means your income minus your expenses equals zero. One more time: Your income minus *everything else* equals zero. That means you give every dollar a job to do—every month. *Hint: That's why we named our tool EveryDollar.* Make a plan on purpose for every dollar, every month!

1 **START WITH YOUR INCOME**

2 **LIST ALL YOUR EXPENSES**

3 **SUBTRACT EXPENSES FROM INCOME**

4 **TRACK YOUR EXPENSES**

5 **BE FLEXIBLE!**

HOW TO DO A MONTHLY BUDGET

1 START WITH YOUR INCOME

Write down all the income you expect for the month.

💳 INCOME	
Paycheck	$3,500

2 LIST ALL YOUR EXPENSES

This is *everything* going out this month, from giving to groceries to miscellaneous!

🏠 EXPENSES	
Giving	$350
Saving	$450
Rent	$875
Utilities	$350
Groceries/Restaurants	$525
Transportation	$350
Insurance	$500
Miscellaneous	$100

3 SUBTRACT EXPENSES FROM INCOME

If your income minus your expenses equals zero, you did it! You've just made a zero-based budget. If it doesn't, you've got some work to do! Adjust some categories and get to zero.

	💳 INCOME
−	🏠 EXPENSES
=	**$0**

4 TRACK YOUR EXPENSES

Track your expenses every day during the month to make sure you're sticking to your budget. If you're overspending, make adjustments in your categories and then learn to say no!

5 BE FLEXIBLE!

Planning for payments shows you just how much debt steals your income! Let's say you have a car payment of $325 and a student loan payment of $150. You need to include those debts in your budget and adjust other categories to account for those expenses. Remember, your income minus *everything else* has to equal zero.

💳 DEBTS	
Car Payment	$325
Student Loan	$150

🏠 EXPENSES	
Saving	$200
Groceries/Restaurants	$300

Updated Totals

BABY STEP 1

As soon as you get $1,000 in the bank, come back to this page and mark the date you officially knocked out Baby Step 1!

⌖ GOAL

$1,000

📅 DATE COMPLETED

_____ / _____ / _____

MONTH   DAY   YEAR

This is the EASIEST and the HARDEST STEP

"Your income is your most **POWERFUL** wealth-building **TOOL.**

— **DAVE RAMSEY**

BABY STEP 2

KEY POINTS

- Baby Step 2 is paying off all debt (except the house) using the debt snowball.

- Debt is not a tool used to build wealth, and payments don't have to be a way of life.

- It takes gazelle intensity to get out of debt.

BABY STEP
2

Pay Off All Debt (Except the House) Using the Debt Snowball

You've got $1,000 in the bank, and you're ready for Baby Step 2: paying off all your debt except your house using the debt snowball! Attack the smallest debt first while making minimum payments on the others. Once you pay off the first one, you'll move to the next smallest debt, taking your freed-up money, newfound motivation and momentum with you—until you pay off the last, largest debt!

LESSON 2 //
BABY STEP 2

GUIDE
Dave Ramsey

BABY STEP 2

Pay off all _____ (except the house) using the debt snowball.

The rich *rule* over the poor, and the borrower is *slave* to the lender.

— PROVERBS 22:7 (NIV)

MYTHS & TRUTHS

MYTH: I need a credit card to rent a car and make purchases online.

TRUTH: You can do both of these things with a _____ card.

....

MYTH: Car payments are a way of life. You can't live without a car payment.

TRUTH: You can stay away from car payments by paying cash for reliable used cars.

....

MYTH: I need to take out a credit card to build up my credit score.

TRUTH: The FICO score is an "I love _____" score.

ANSWER KEY

Debt
Debit
Debt

LESSON 2 //
MYTHS & TRUTHS

MYTH: I pay my credit card off every month. And I can earn points and airline miles.

TRUTH: When you use a credit card instead of cash, you actually spend _____ because you don't feel it.

....

MYTH: A credit card is more secure than a debit card.

TRUTH: Debit cards and credit cards have the _____ amount of protection.

....

MYTH: My teenager needs a credit card to learn how to be responsible with money.

TRUTH: More students drop out of school because of _____ trouble than for academic failure.

....

MYTH: Leasing a car is smart. You should always lease things that go down in value. There are tax advantages.

TRUTH: Consumer Reports and a good calculator will tell you that a car _____ is the most expensive way to operate and finance a vehicle.

....

MYTH: I can get a good deal on a new car.

TRUTH: A new car loses _____% of its value in the first five years.

ANSWER KEY

More
Same
Financial
Lease
60

34 // Lesson 2

LESSON 2 //
MYTHS & TRUTHS

MYTH: A home equity loan is a good option for consolidation and a great substitute for an emergency fund.

TRUTH: You don't go into debt when you're in the middle of an emergency. You'll make the emergency a _____.

....

MYTH: Debt consolidation is smart. It saves interest and gets you a smaller payment.

TRUTH: Debt consolidation does nothing to change the _____ that got you into debt. So, many who do it actually end up with more debt.

....

MYTH: Cosigning a loan is okay if I'm helping a friend or relative.

TRUTH: The bank requires a cosigner because the person isn't likely to _____.

....

MYTH: You can't go to college without taking out student loans.

TRUTH: _____% of millionaires with a college degree never took out student loans.

ANSWER KEY

Crisis
Behavior
Repay
68

LESSON 2 //
MYTHS & TRUTHS

BIGGEST MYTH OF ALL

MYTH: Debt is a tool and should be used to create prosperity.

TRUTH: Debt is proof that the borrower is _____ to the lender.

Give *no sleep* to your eyes, nor slumber to your eyelids. Deliver yourself *like a gazelle* from the hand of the hunter, and like a bird from the hand of the fowler.

— PROVERBS 6:4–5 (NKJV)

NOTES

_____

_____

_____

_____

_____

_____

ANSWER KEY
Slave

LESSON 2 //
DEBT SNOWBALL

HOW TO GET OUT OF DEBT

- Quit borrowing more _____!

- You must _____ money.

- _____ something.

- Take a part-time _____.

- _____ really works.

DEBT SNOWBALL

List your debts smallest to largest. Make minimum payments on all of them and attack the smallest one with a vengeance.

One-Minute TAKEAWAY

ANSWER KEY

Money
Save
Sell
Job
Prayer

IT'S TIME FOR A PLASECTOMY

Remember, your situation will never change until you do! So, grab the scissors and slash your lifeline to stupid. You're done with debt and you're never going back, which means you're done with credit cards. That's right. It's time for a plasectomy.

We get it. This step is hard. But debt has taken too much from you already. And it's the biggest thief of your financial future. So, get the cards out of your life and start attacking debt with a vengeance! Goodbye, credit cards. Hello, freedom.

Whether you cut them up in your class or at home on your own, **write down the card information first**! Once you pay them off, you'll have to call and cancel each account.

	CREDIT CARD NAME	PLASECTOMY DATE	CANCEL DATE
1			
2			
3			
4			
5			
6			
7			

HOW TO CLOSE OUT YOUR
CREDIT CARDS

The plasectomy is a mental and physical sign that you're done with debt—forever. *No more. No way. No how.* But there are **three steps** to breaking up with your credit cards for good!

❶ PAY OFF THE BALANCE

Go ahead and cut up the cards. But before you can cancel the accounts, you'll need to pay off the balance. No matter how much you have to pay off, just list the payments in your debt snowball and attack them with gazelle intensity one by one!

❷ CALL THE CREDIT CARD COMPANY

Once you pay off the balance, call the credit card company and say, "I'm calling to close my account." Spoiler alert: They're going to say whatever they can think of to keep you from leaving. Don't fall for their gimmicks or counteroffers. Just repeat, "I'm calling to close my account." Be firm, and remember, you're *done* with debt.

❸ GET IT IN WRITING

When you call to cancel your account, keep a record of the conversation's details. You'll want written proof from the company that your account is clear and closed. It's also a good idea to check your credit report later in the year to verify that these accounts are actually closed.

DISCUSSION

Whether you're in a class or online, be honest with your answers and remember to encourage one another!

 Look over the list of myths and truths Dave covered in the video. Which myths have fooled you in the past? How can you make sure you don't get duped again?

 What fears or concerns do you have about living without credit cards?

 Proverbs 22:7 says that "the borrower is slave to the lender" (NIV). What would your life look like if you were totally debt-free? What could you do that you can't afford to do now?

 Dave says, "You can wander into debt, but you can't wander out." You'll have to make some tough decisions and sacrifices moving forward. What's one area you can cut back—or cut out—to reach your money goals?

 You need serious passion and motivation to get out of debt. What's one thing you can do to kick-start and keep up your gazelle intensity?

ACTION STEPS

It's time to live out what you just learned! Complete each of the Action Steps before the next lesson.

☐ **CUT UP YOUR CREDIT CARDS**
If you didn't do it as part of the Activity, gather the family, grab scissors, and host a plasectomy party! This is when you decide to stop the crazy cycle of debt—so celebrate! Just remember that you'll also need to call each credit card company and close the accounts once and for all.

☐ **FILL OUT YOUR DEBT SNOWBALL**
If you have any non-mortgage debts, list them in your debt snowball in **Ramsey+**. We'll help you sort your debts from smallest to largest so you can start attacking the first one right away. Make sure you track your payoff progress in **Ramsey+** so you always know how close you are to your debt-free date! Don't have any debt? Head to the next Action Step!

☐ **GET GAZELLE INTENSE**
If you're in Baby Step 1, 2 or 3, it's time to get intense—this is a "whatever it takes" mentality! That means you pause investing, sell the second TV, ban restaurants, and work overtime. A couple years of intense sacrifice is worth a lifetime of freedom.

☐ **TRACK YOUR TRANSACTIONS IN EVERYDOLLAR**
Actually using your budget is the only way it will work for you! Stay on budget by tracking your transactions and dragging them into the right categories. That's how you'll see exactly how much you've spent in each category you budgeted for! **Pro tip:** Connect your bank to **EveryDollar** so your transactions show up in your budget automatically.

☐ **READ "THE DEBT SNOWBALL" ON THE NEXT PAGE**
Need a reminder on how the debt snowball works? Check out how this method is the fastest way to get rid of debt!

THE DEBT *Snowball*

What could you do if you didn't owe anyone your paycheck? That means no student loans, no credit card bills, no car payments—no debt. With the **debt snowball**, you'll pay off the smallest debt first and work your way up to the largest. *But wait.* Doesn't it make sense mathematically to pay off the debt with the highest interest rate first? Maybe. But if you'd been paying attention to math, you wouldn't be in debt. It's time to pay attention to your behavior. Enter the debt snowball.

Attack!

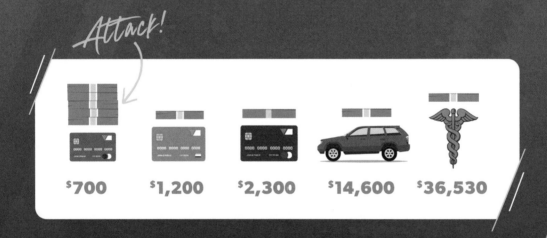

$700 $1,200 $2,300 $14,600 $36,530

1 **LIST YOUR DEBTS FROM SMALLEST TO LARGEST**
Don't worry about the interest rates! Seriously—smallest to largest.

2 **ATTACK THE SMALLEST DEBT WITH A VENGEANCE**
Make minimum payments on all your other debts while you pay off the smallest debt as fast as you can!

3 REPEAT THIS METHOD AS YOU PLOW YOUR WAY THROUGH EACH DEBT

Once that debt is gone, take its payment and apply it to the next-smallest debt. The more you pay off, the more your freed-up money grows and gets thrown onto the next debt—like a snowball rolling downhill.

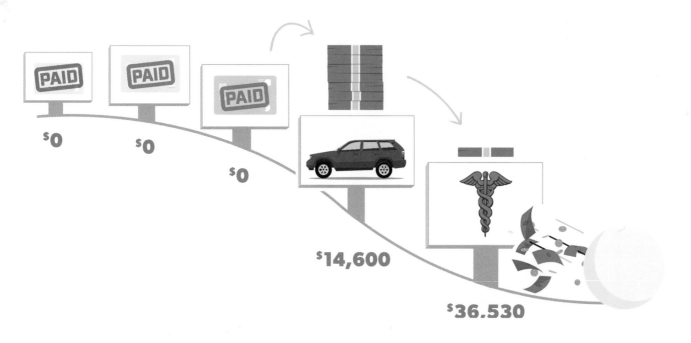

$0

$0

$0

$14,600

$36.530

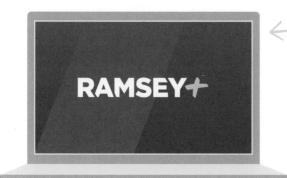

TRACK YOUR PROGRESS IN RAMSEY+

Complete your debt snowball and track your progress as you pay off debt!

BABY STEP 2

Take the total number from your debt snowball and write it below. Then, once you pay off that very last debt, celebrate and come back to this page to mark the day you became debt-free.

🎯 GOAL

$

📅 DATE COMPLETED

_____ / _____ / _____

MONTH   DAY   YEAR

YOU CAN *Wander* INTO DEBT, BUT YOU *Can't* WANDER OUT

An **EMERGENCY FUND**
takes the drama out of life.

— **GEORGE KAMEL**

BABY STEP 3

KEY POINTS

- Baby Step 3 is saving 3–6 months of expenses in a fully funded emergency fund.

- The emergency fund is Murphy repellent. It keeps you from living in fear of the next emergency.

- Your emergency fund is insurance, not an investment! It prevents you from going back into debt.

BABY STEP

3

Save 3–6 Months of Expenses in a Fully Funded Emergency Fund

Baby Step 3 is all about building your full emergency fund with 3–6 months of expenses. After the momentum and intensity of Baby Step 2, it's easy to let your foot off the gas. Don't let that happen! Keep your intensity through Baby Step 3. In the same way your $1,000 starter emergency fund kept you from going into debt because of emergency expenses, your fully funded emergency fund will protect you when life's bigger surprises hit.

LESSON 3 //
SAVING

GUIDE
Rachel Cruze

SAVING

" **Debt** *steals* **your future.**
Saving *secures* **it.** "

— RACHEL CRUZE

Nearly 80% of Americans live paycheck to paycheck. They use _____ to cover emergencies.

The emergency fund gives you _____ to cover emergencies so you stay out of debt.

You can save money if it's your _____.

The wise man *saves* for the future, but the foolish man *spends* whatever he gets.

— PROVERBS 21:20 (TLB)

The _____ for comparison is contentment.

_____ will lead you to contentment.

LESSON 3 //
SAVING

GUIDE
George Kamel

I am not saying this because I am in need, for I have *learned* to be *content* whatever the circumstances.

— **PHILIPPIANS 4:11** (NIV)

BABY STEP 3

Save _____ months of expenses in a fully funded emergency fund.

Murphy's Law states: Anything that can go wrong _____ go wrong.

Save _____ months of expenses if you fall into any of these categories:

- You're married but have a single-income household.

- You're a single parent.

- You or your spouse is self-employed, work on commission, or have a highly irregular income.

- Your job is seasonal.

- You or someone in your household is chronically ill.

ANSWER KEY
3–6
Will
Six

For *wisdom* provides protection, just as *money* provides protection.

— ECCLESIASTES 7:12 (NET)

Save at least _____ months of expenses if you fall into either of these categories:

- You're single with no dependents and a stable income.

- You're married and have two incomes, both of which are stable.

An emergency fund is _____. It's not an investment.

When you use your emergency fund, _____ it back up.

One-Minute TAKEAWAY

_____

_____

_____

_____

ANSWER KEY

Three
Insurance
Build

Stay GAZELLE INTENSE

Let's look at two couples. We'll call them Brian & Heather and Ashton & Kelsey.

Both couples were gazelle intense and made extreme sacrifices to pay off their debt. They're finally debt-free! Baby Step 2—check! They take a few weeks to breathe and celebrate before they dive into Baby Step 3.

But now, they're ready to get their **fully funded emergency fund** up and running! They look at their current savings and expenses and decide on their emergency fund goal.

HERE ARE THEIR *Numbers*

$1,000

CURRENT EMERGENCY FUND

$2,000

CURRENT MONTHLY EXPENSES

Both couples are single-income households and need a six-month emergency fund!

$12,000

FULLY FUNDED EMERGENCY FUND GOAL

HOW TO SAVE FOR BABY STEP 3

With $1,000 already in the bank from Baby Step 1, how many months will it take each couple to reach their $12,000 goal?

BRIAN & HEATHER

ASHTON & KELSEY

Brian & Heather continue celebrating and let off the gas. They only put **$300 per month** into their emergency fund.

Ashton & Kelsey stay gazelle intense and put the **$1,000 per month** that *was* going toward debt right into their emergency fund.

MONTHS

MONTHS

Moral of the story? **Don't let off the gas!** Take what you were throwing at debt and save it in your fully funded emergency fund. Keep up your gazelle intensity through Baby Step 3!

Respond to the following questions:

 1. Remember to stay gazelle intense in Baby Step 3. But what's the one way you'll celebrate being debt-free before you kick it back into high gear?

 2. If these couples asked you about investing or paying off their mortgage before completing Baby Step 3, what advice would you give them? Why?

DISCUSSION

Whether you're taking this class online or in person, be honest with your answers and remember to encourage one another!

 By now, you've seen and experienced the power of the debt snowball. How can its momentum help you knock out your emergency fund? Why is that important to know?

 When have you wished you had Murphy repellent in your life? How would a fully funded emergency fund have turned that crisis into a simple inconvenience?

 In building your emergency fund, consider the suggested savings range of 3–6 months of expenses. Which amount makes the most sense for your life and gives you the most peace?

 Once you're debt-free, it can be tempting to let your foot off the gas and taper off the intensity. But we want you to move through the first three Baby Steps as fast as you can! What are some practical things you can do to maintain your gazelle intensity in Baby Step 3?

ACTION STEPS

It's time to live out what you just learned! Complete each of the Action Steps before the next lesson.

☐ **CALCULATE YOUR BABY STEP 3 GOAL**
It's time to protect yourself from Murphy! Before you can save 3–6 months of expenses, you need to figure out how much you need to save. First, determine if you need three or six months of expenses saved. (Look back at the lesson for a quick reminder.) Second, multiply that number by how much you spend on essential expenses each month. And just like that, you've got your Baby Step 3 goal.

☐ **OPEN A SEPARATE ACCOUNT**
No matter which Baby Step you're on, make sure your emergency fund is in a separate account from your checking account! It needs to be easy for you to get to, but not too easy to spend from. Here are some options: a savings account connected to your checking account, a money market account that comes with a debit card or check-writing privileges, or an online bank where you can transfer money quickly and directly to your checking account.

☐ **TRACK YOUR TRANSACTIONS IN EVERYDOLLAR**
Make sure you're sticking to the budget you set by tracking your transactions. If you connected your bank to **EveryDollar**, this takes minutes—just drag and drop the transactions into the right budget lines, and you're done. **Pro tip:** This is also a great time to make any edits to your budget lines and see where you're accidentally overspending.

☐ **READ "EXACTLY HOW MUCH DO YOU SAVE FOR BABY STEP 3?" ON THE NEXT PAGE**
Want to see a real example of how to calculate your Baby Step 3 goal? Check out the next page!

EXACTLY HOW MUCH DO YOU SAVE FOR BABY STEP 3?

Remember the budget Rachel created in Lesson 1? Our example couple was budgeting for the very first time so they could cut expenses and save $1,000 ASAP. Well, guess what? It's been two years, and they just made their final debt payment (cue the confetti!). Now, they're ready to start saving their fully funded emergency fund in Baby Step 3!

How will they figure out the exact number they need to save? With the same three easy steps you'll follow:

1 **DETERMINE** if you (and your spouse, if you're married) need three or six months of expenses saved.

2 **GET YOUR BUDGET OUT** and add up how much you're spending on giving and essential expenses each month. (FYI, EveryDollar totals this for you!)

3 **MULTIPLY** your answer for #1 by your total for #2.

THAT'S YOUR BABY STEP 3 *Savings Goal!*

INCOME

Paychecks	$5,700
Side Hustle	$600

EXPENSES

Giving	$630
Mortgage/Rent	$1,250
Electric	$100
Water	$60
Natural Gas	$30
Transportation	$250
Groceries	$600
Miscellaneous	$201
Mom Fun Money	$50
Dad Fun Money	$50
Haircuts	$40
Christmas	$25
Birthdays	$25
Childcare	$700
Cell Phones	$70
Internet	$60
Clothing	$50
Ramsey+ Membership	$11
Media/Music	$35
Doctor Visits	$40
Insurance	$100
~~Student Loan~~	~~$1,923~~

$4,377
Spent

Let's follow along with our example couple to see how they walk through each step.

1 Both Mom and Dad have stable jobs, so according to George, they should save **three months** of expenses.

2 They take out their EveryDollar budget and see that last month, they spent $4,377. (Remember, debt will no longer come out of their paychecks, so they don't need to plan for it in their expenses.) Then, they talk through items they won't need *every* month, like haircuts and new clothes. So, they look at what they spent on average over the last three months and land on **$4,200**.

3 Finally, they get out their calculator and punch in 3 x 4,200 = **$12,600**.

THEIR BABY STEP 3 SAVINGS GOAL IS
$12,600

Since they already have $1,000 in their emergency fund from Baby Step 1, they need to save **$11,600** to get it fully funded.

Now they ask, "How fast can we save $11,600 to finish Baby Step 3?"

Great news! Since they got gazelle intense in Baby Step 2 by living on a budget and working a side hustle, they were able to pay **$1,923** toward debt last month.

If they keep up their intensity, they can *save* $1,923 per month (since they aren't *sending* it to Sallie Mae anymore), and they'll be done with Baby Step 3 in **six months**. (P.S. The math on that is: $11,600 savings goal ÷ $1,923 payment = 6 months!)

They're done with debt!

BABY STEP 3

Write your Baby Step 3 goal below and bookmark this page. On the day you save your last dollar in Baby Step 3, you'll see how all your hard work paid off!

🎯 GOAL

$

📅 DATE COMPLETED

_____ / _____ / _____

MONTH   DAY   YEAR

AN *Emergency* FUND TURNS A CRISIS INTO AN *Inconvenience*

"

This is a
WEALTH-BUILDING
plan, not just a get-out-
of-debt plan.

— DAVE RAMSEY

"

BABY STEPS 4 5 6 7

KEY POINTS

- Baby Step 4 is to invest 15% of your household income in retirement.

- Baby Step 5 is to save for your children's college fund.

- Baby Step 6 is to pay off your home early.

- Baby Step 7 is to build wealth and give.

- You'll do Baby Steps 4–6 in order, but at the same time. Then, Baby Step 7 is where you'll have the most fun!

BABY STEP

4

Invest 15% of Your Household Income in Retirement

You've finished paying for the past—now it's time to start paying for your future! On Baby Step 4, you'll invest 15% of your household income into tax-advantaged accounts for retirement. There is no quick-fix, snap-your-fingers way to build wealth, but you *can* become a Baby Steps Millionaire. The key is to start investing early and consistently, letting compound interest work its magic!

LESSON 4 //
BABY STEP 4

GUIDE
Dave Ramsey

When you follow the Baby Steps over time, you _____ become a Baby Steps Millionaire.

MILLIONAIRE MYTHS & TRUTHS

MYTH: Millionaires inherit their wealth.

TRUTH: 89% of millionaires are not millionaires because of inheritance. In fact, 79% received _____ inheritance.

MYTH: Millionaires have high salaries.

TRUTH: 33% of millionaires _____ earned more than $100,000 in any single working year of their career.

A faithful man will abound with *blessings,* but he who hastens to be rich will *not go unpunished.*

— **PROVERBS 28:20** (NKJV)

MYTH: Millionaires follow a get-rich-quick method.

TRUTH: _____% of millionaires attribute regular, consistent investing in retirement plans over a long period of time as a reason for their success.

ANSWER KEY
Will
Zero
Never
79

LESSON 4 //
BABY STEP 4

MYTH: Millionaires take risks when investing and play the stock market.

TRUTH: _____% of millionaires reached millionaire status through their employer-sponsored retirement plan.

Wealth gained *hastily* will dwindle, but whoever gathers *little by little* will increase it.

— PROVERBS 13:11 (ESV)

MYTH: Millionaires get the best rate of return on their investments.

TRUTH: Rates of return, asset allocation and expense ratios on investments only account for _____% or less of a millionaire's success.

NOTES

ANSWER KEY
80
20

LESSON 4 //
BABY STEP 4

BABY STEP 4

Baby Step 4 is to invest _____% of your household income in retirement.

Investing $_____ every month from age 25 to age 65 (at an 11% rate of return) gets you to $1.3 million.

Have a _____ meeting with your spouse. If you're single, talk with your accountability partner.

The secret to becoming a Baby Steps Millionaire is _____ you can do it.

Numbers change when _____ do.

NOTES

The Story of
JACK & BLAKE
AND THE POWER OF COMPOUND GROWTH

JACK

At age 21, Jack decided to invest $2,400 every year ($200 per month) for nine years. Then, at age 30, Jack stopped putting money into his investments. So all together, he put a total of $21,600 into his investment funds, then left them alone.

BLAKE

Blake didn't start investing until age 30—nine years after Jack got started. And just like Jack, Blake put $2,400 into his investment funds every year—but he invested 29 more years than Jack. Blake invested a total of $91,200 over 38 years.

At age 67, Jack and Blake decided to compare their investment accounts. Who do you think had more? Jack, with his total of $21,600 invested over nine years, or Blake, who invested $91,200 over 38 years? Check this out:

Jack starts investing money at 21 years old.

$0 $0 $0 $0 $0 $0 $0 $0 $0 $0 $0 $0

$0 $0 $0 $0 $0 $0 $0 $0 $0

21 • • • • • • **30** • • • • • • **40** • •

Blake starts investing money at 30 years old.

JACK

Total invested over 9 years:
$21,600

Return:
$2,547,150

He never caught up!

BLAKE

Total invested over 38 years:
$91,200

Return:
$1,483,033

$0 $0 $0 $0 $0 $0 $0 $0 $0 $0 $0 $0 $0 $0 $0 $0 $0 $0 $0 $0

50 • • • • • • **60** • • • • • **67**

Blake invests $2,400 a year through
age 67—almost his entire life.

THE MORAL OF THE STORY IS **START EARLY!**

BABY STEP

5

Save for Your Children's College Fund

By this step, you've paid off all your debt except the house and you've started saving for retirement. Now it's time to save for your children's college expenses using an Education Savings Account (ESA) or a 529 plan. Help your children go to college the right way—without debt. It *can* be done!

LESSON 4 //
BABY STEP 5

GUIDE
Rachel Cruze

BABY STEP 5

Save for your children's _____ fund.

You have two options for college savings—an _____
and a _____ plan.

Train up a *child* in the way he
should go, and when he is old
he will not *depart* from it.

— **PROVERBS 22:6** (NKJV)

Three ways to go to college debt-free:

1. Select an _____ school.

2. _____ for things like scholarships, grants
    and work study.

3. Get a _____.

"**College is a blessing, not
an *entitlement*.**"

— **RACHEL CRUZE**

BABY STEP

6

Pay Off Your Home Early

Baby Step 6 is the big one! There's only one more thing standing in the way of your complete freedom from debt—your mortgage. This part of paying off debt is a little more like a marathon. But any extra money you can put toward your mortgage will help save you tens of thousands of dollars in interest. And the grass will truly feel different under your feet once it's *yours*.

LESSON 4 //
BABY STEP 6

GUIDE
Dave Ramsey

BABY STEP 6

Pay off your home _____.

100% of foreclosures occur on a home with

a _____.

Should you **PAY OFF YOUR HOME EARLY?**

INTEREST vs. TAXES

The interest you pay on your mortgage is deductible on your taxes. Are you saving more money by taking this deduction or should you just pay the taxes? Let's take a look.

MORTGAGE INTEREST

$200K   x   5%   = $10,000

MORTGAGE AMOUNT   INTEREST RATE   ANNUAL INTEREST PAID

TAXES WITH PAID HOME

$10K   x   22%   = $2,200

TAXABLE AMOUNT   TAX BRACKET   TAXES PAID

SO, WHAT MAKES MORE SENSE . . .

PAYING $10,000 TO A BANK OR PAYING $2,200 TO THE IRS?

BABY STEP

7

Build Wealth and Give

You know what people with no debt and no payments can do? Anything they want! Now you can truly live and give like no one else by building wealth, becoming insanely generous, and changing your family tree. Your focus and sacrifice got you here. You made it. You lived like no one else, and now you get to *live* and *give* like no one else!

LESSON 4 //
BABY STEP 7

GUIDE
Dave Ramsey

BABY STEP 7

Build wealth and be outrageously _____ !

Giving is possibly the most _____ you will ever have with money.

Each of you should *give* what you have decided in your heart to give, not reluctantly or under compulsion, for God loves a *cheerful giver.*

— 2 CORINTHIANS 9:7 (NIV)

ANSWER KEY

Generous
Fun

Dream FOR YOUR FUTURE

You wake up to silence and sun. There's no alarm clock ringing in your ear. In fact, there's no clock in your bedroom at all. You reach for your phone out of habit and put it back on your nightstand before rolling over in bed. **There's a lot you used to do that you don't have to do anymore.**

You don't check your **inbox**—you couldn't, even if you wanted to. You retired years ago, long before your coworkers.

You don't check **social media** when you first wake up. You quit the comparison game back when you learned the power of contentment. Plus, you're living your dream. You don't want someone else's life—you love yours.

You don't check your **bank account**. You know how much you have . . . you even know your net worth. You hit seven figures when you became a Baby Steps Millionaire.

You don't check a list of what you must do. You get to list what you want to do. **So, what do you want to do?**

WHAT'S YOUR DREAM RETIREMENT?

Get specific! Want to travel? Write where you want to go. Want to live closer to your kids? Jot down what your dream home looks like. Want to start a business? Put it on paper!

> I'm not sure of if I will enjoy traveling as much as I do now so its hard to say but I'll like to start an artist residency somewhere beautiful and dramatic like that British artist Tracey emin

IT'S TIME TO LIVE AND GIVE LIKE NO ONE ELSE

Picture this: You're living your dream retirement! You're traveling the way you always wanted. You're spending more time with your kids—and maybe even your grandkids. You own your home. And it's not just any house on the block. It's your dream home.

You've worked hard for years and years to get to where you are today. And it was all worth it.

YOU'RE ON BABY STEP 7!

Now you get to have some serious fun with money.

 You just heard Dave tell the story of his friend who took his entire family on a cruise. **How will you have fun spending your money?**

Not sure yet

You also heard Dave tell the story of this same friend taking his entire family to give bikes away to kids in need. **How will you have fun giving your money?**

Interdiciplinay Artist resiency funded like tracey Emin

DISCUSSION

Whether you're in a class or online, be honest with your answers and remember to encourage one another!

 Before this lesson, did you believe it was possible for you to become a millionaire? How has this lesson changed the way you think about building wealth and dreaming about your future?

 If you're a parent, how do you feel about investing for retirement before saving for your children's college fund? Based on the ages of your kids, what is your plan to send them to college debt-free?

 If you're currently paying a mortgage each month, how would paying off your home early change your life? What would you be able to do that you can't do now?

 When is a time that generosity has impacted your life? Were you the giver or the receiver?

ACTION STEPS

It's time to live out what you just learned! Complete each of the Action Steps before the next lesson.

☐ **SCHEDULE A BUDGET COMMITTEE MEETING**
You're coming up on your next budgeting cycle! Remember, it takes three months to get the budget right, so stick with it. If you're married, schedule your next Budget Committee Meeting. Singles, don't forget to review your budget with your accountability partner. And keep tracking your transactions!

☐ **MAKE SURE GIVING IS AT THE TOP OF YOUR BUDGET**
When you hold money with an open hand—not a clenched fist—you're able to give generously *and* receive graciously. No matter which Baby Step you're on, giving is your priority, whether that's a tithe to your church or contributions to charity.

☐ **KNOW YOUR NET WORTH**
Your net worth is what you own (assets) minus what you owe (liabilities). It's an overall measure of wealth. Use the Net Worth Calculator in **Ramsey+** to see where you stand today!

☐ **CONTACT A SMARTVESTOR PRO**
If you're done with Baby Step 3, check out our list of SmartVestor Pros near you in **Ramsey+**. These investing professionals will help you invest the right way for you and learn how to save for your kids' college.

☐ **READ "IN ORDER, BUT AT THE SAME TIME" ON THE NEXT PAGE**
The Baby Steps work when you do them in order. But Baby Steps 4–6 are done at the same time! We know that sounds confusing, but this Deep Dive tells you exactly what we mean.

BABY STEPS 4 5 6

IN ORDER, BUT AT THE SAME TIME

You do Baby Steps 1, 2 and 3 one at a time. Check. You do Baby Steps 4, 5 and 6 at the same time. *What?*

Baby Steps 1, 2 and 3 require laser focus and gazelle intensity—and they each have a specific dollar goal. After Baby Step 3, however, the plan changes gears. You'll do Baby Steps 4, 5 and 6 in order, but at the same time.

Here's what we mean:

Meet the Campbells.

This average American family has a household income of $5,000 per month. They used the debt snowball to put $1,500 a month toward paying off all their debt. Then they used the *same* gazelle intensity and saved $1,500 a month to finish their emergency fund.

The Campbells celebrate! They get to ease up on their intensity some, but they're ready to attack **Baby Steps 4, 5 and 6—in order, but at the same time**.

IF THEY SET ASIDE $1,000 FOR THESE BABY STEPS, WATCH WHAT WOULD HAPPEN:

1 **START BABY STEP 4**

The Campbells save 15% of their gross income in retirement. So, they open a Roth 401(k) and start investing $750 every month.

4 Roth 401(k): **$750**

$250 left to budget

---

2 **START BABY STEP 5**

They open an ESA for their 3-year-old and contribute $166 per month. (That's the ESA contribution limit as of 2022.)

4 Roth 401(k): **$750**　　**5** ESA: **$166**

$84 left to budget

---

3 **START BABY STEP 6**

The Campbells still have $84! They go ahead and add it to their mortgage payment knowing they could find more money in the budget to throw at their home if they wanted to.

4 Roth 401(k): **$750**　　**5** ESA: **$166**　　**6** Extra on home: **$84**

$0 left to budget!

There you have it. Baby Steps 4, 5 and 6—**IN ORDER, BUT AT THE SAME TIME.**

Make sure what you BUY aligns with the person you WANT to be.

— GEORGE KAMEL

WISE
SPENDING

KEY POINTS

- There are a million marketing tactics trying to go after your money and bust your budget.

- When you spend wisely, you can have power over purchases.

- More stuff won't make you more complete.

LESSON 5 //
WISE SPENDING

GUIDE
Dr. John Delony

When faced with a threat, our brain generally responds in one of three ways: fight, flight or _____.

Our brains are constantly asking _____ questions:

1. Am I safe?

2. Do I belong?

3. Does it feel good?

Marketers and neuroscientists know you better than _____ do.

You're more likely to buy something when you're _____.

You can take your _____ back.

NOTES

LESSON 5 //
WISE SPENDING

GUIDE
George Kamel

6 WAYS COMPANIES GO AFTER OUR MONEY

1. **Personal Selling**

   Salespeople are trained to convince you to _____.

2. **Product Placement**

   Companies _____ to have their products placed strategically.

3. **Brand Association**

   The products you buy tell a _____ about you.

4. **Sales and Promotions**

   Never spend just to _____.

5. **Convenient Payment Methods**

   Making a purchase has become so easy that spending money is _____.

6. **Financing**

   When you _____, you're asking, "How much down? How much a month?" Wise spenders ask, "How much?"

ANSWER KEY

Buy
Pay
Story
Save
Painless
Finance

"**Don't let discounts drive** *decisions.*"

— GEORGE KAMEL

LESSON 5 //
WISE SPENDING

GEORGE'S SMART SPENDER GUIDE

Self-Awareness

Will this add _____ to my life?

Motive

Am I buying this for the _____ reason?

Affordability

Is this in my _____?

Research

Is this the _____ option, retailer and price?

Timing

Is _____ the time to buy it?

You can't _____ your way into a meaningful life.

One-Minute TAKEAWAY

_____

_____

_____

_____

_____

_____

ANSWER KEY

Value
Right
Budget
Best
Now
Spend

TIME TO GET
HONEST
WITH *Yourself*

We've all bought something we didn't need with money we didn't plan to spend—or worse, with money we didn't have. In this Activity, we've listed the six common ways companies go after our money. It's time to get honest with yourself: Think about a time when these methods have influenced you to make a purchase, and fill out the chart. If you're married, share your answers with your spouse.

Marketing Method	Have these methods influenced you to make a purchase? Yes or no? Explain your answer.
Personal Selling	Y N _____
Product Placement	Y N _____
Brand Association	Y N _____
Sales and Promotions	Y N _____
Convenient Payment Methods	Y N _____
Financing	Y N _____

Respond to the following question:

 1. Marketing isn't evil (except financing—that's always a bad idea), but to be a wise spender, you need to see when it's happening and think before you spend! What did this Activity reveal about your spending habits?

DISCUSSION

Whether you're taking the class online or in person, be honest with your answers and remember to encourage one another!

 1 When was the last time you made an emotional purchase (from stress, fear, sadness, distraction, etc.)? What was it (tacos, shoes, concert tickets, matching sweaters for you and your dog, etc.)?

 2 What's a moment when comparison crept in and affected your spending?

 3 What's the worst impulse purchase you've ever made? Why was it so bad? How would you do things differently next time?

 4 Can you think of the last targeted ad you got? What was it for? Did it influence you to make a purchase?

 5 How can you get into the habit of walking through George's SMART Spender method rather than making an emotional or impulse purchase?

ACTION STEPS

It's time to live out what you just learned! Complete each of the Action Steps before the next lesson.

☐ **CREATE YOUR SECOND BUDGET WITH EVERYDOLLAR**
You wrapped up your first month of budgeting—that's a huge accomplishment! Don't get hung up on how many mistakes you made or if you feel like your first budget didn't work. It usually takes three months of budgeting for things to really click. So, learn from your first budget and go create your second budget with EveryDollar.

☐ **TRACK YOUR TRANSACTIONS IN EVERYDOLLAR**
Stick to the budget you create by tracking your transactions every week. Remember, when your bank is connected to EveryDollar, this is a super simple process—just drag and drop your transactions into the right categories and you're done!

☐ **COMMIT TO CASH**
Use George's SMART Spender guide, follow your budget, and commit to cash so you aren't racking up payments every time you want to buy something. Bottom line? Don't buy anything you can't afford. Don't Afterpay for it—actually pay for it. This week, commit to ditching credit cards and payment plans!

☐ **READ "HOW TO BE A SMART SPENDER" ON THE NEXT PAGE**
Overspending, impulse spending and unwise spending are some of the biggest traps for buyers! Now that you've learned about George's SMART Spender guide, it's time to see how you'd use this guide in action.

HOW TO BE A *Smart* SPENDER

It's Saturday, and for Jordan, that means no work and no big to-dos! She's up for a little shopping and has her eye on an air fryer and a new smartphone.

Jordan's ready to snag a deal (or two), but she also learned from George and wants to be a wise spender—there's no reason to bust her budget or derail her plan for items she wants but doesn't need. So, she does a quick online search for the two items she wants and walks herself through the **SMART Spender questions** from this lesson.

Let's step into her thinking and see if she decides it's wise to buy either of these two items!

AIR FRYER

S SELF-AWARENESS
Will this add value to my life?
Yes. I'm trying to cook more at home to save money, and this will help me meal prep faster, with less mess and stress.

M MOTIVE
Am I buying this for the right reason?
Hm. I did think about getting one because several friends at work mentioned how great air fryers are. But I'm not trying to be like them. I really want this time-saving, money-saving tool for what it is!

A AFFORDABILITY
Is this in my budget?
Yes! I've been saving for more kitchen appliances, and I've got enough to pay in full!

R RESEARCH
**Is this the best option,
retailer and price?**
It is. I narrowed down which kind I wanted,
and after a quick search of other sales
today, I discovered that this one is the
best price.

T TIMING
Is now the time to buy it?
Yup. I've been watching prices for about a
month, and this is the best deal I've seen.

> **Decision:** Jordan clicks Add to Cart. And
> she's guilt-free in her purchase and excited
> to start making crispy chicken nuggets.

Next up, Jordan pulls up the page for the
new smartphone she's been eyeing. Let's
see if this is a wise purchase.

NEW SMARTPHONE

S SELF-AWARENESS
Will this add value to my life?
Well, yeah. Sort of. I'd get a better camera
and faster internet! Plus, they brought
back my favorite color.

*Jordan could probably stop here and decide
this is not the wisest purchase for her right now,
but she asks every question just to be sure!*

M MOTIVE
Am I buying this for the right reason?
To be honest, probably not. My phone
works well. The battery is good. I just want
the new one because there is a new one.
And my friends all got this one.

A AFFORDABILITY
Is this in my budget?
It would be a stretch. Maybe I could cut
back on my Miscellaneous category or
groceries, but that feels risky. I could say
no to the air fryer, but I'd still be short and
things would be tight.

*If Jordan hadn't already said no to this
purchase, she definitely should now! Never
prioritize a want over a need, like groceries!
But let's keep going and see what happens.*

R RESEARCH
**Is this the best option,
retailer and price?**
Yes. It's a great price for this version of
the phone.

T TIMING
Is now the time to buy it?
It's on sale, but I don't need one right now.
I have a perfectly good smartphone.

> **Decision:** Jordan doesn't buy the
> smartphone. She's a little disappointed at
> first. But she didn't budget for it, and she
> realizes it doesn't matter what her friends
> do with their money. She's doing what's
> best for her, and she's proud of her wise
> spending. Jordan's a SMART spender!

Insurance PROTECTS the things that will make you wealthy.

— DAVE RAMSEY

UNDERSTANDING INSURANCE

KEY POINTS

- The purpose of insurance is simply to transfer risk—this is your defensive game plan.

- There are eight types of insurance you actually need.

- No exceptions and no excuses—everyone 18 or older needs a written will.

LESSON 6 //
UNDERSTANDING INSURANCE

GUIDE
Dave Ramsey

THE ROLE OF INSURANCE

The purpose of insurance is to transfer _____ that we can't handle ourselves.

INSURANCES TO AVOID

- Credit life insurance and credit disability insurance on debt you owe

- Mortgage life insurance

- Double indemnity for accidental death

- Cancer insurance

- Prepaid burial insurance

- Return of premium

- Waiver of premium

- Dental and vision insurance

AUTO INSURANCE

If you have a full emergency fund in place, think _____ deductibles.

For _____ coverage on your auto insurance, you want three things: collision, comprehensive and liability.

ANSWER KEY

Risk
High
Full

LESSON 6 //
UNDERSTANDING
INSURANCE

HOMEOWNERS AND RENTERS INSURANCE

You want enough _____ insurance to:

- Rebuild your home (extended dwelling coverage)

- Replace your stuff (personal property)

- Cover injuries and damages that happen on your property (liability)

- Reimburse your living expenses after the loss of an insured home (additional living expenses)

If you're renting, _____ get renters insurance.

NOTES

ANSWER KEY

Homeowners
Always

UMBRELLA POLICY

You need an _____ policy if you have a net worth of at least half a million dollars.

HEALTH INSURANCE

With a traditional health insurance plan, _____ your deductible and/or coinsurance amount to bring your premiums down.

A Health Savings Account (HSA) works with a high-deductible health plan, and you can pay for medical expenses _____-_____.

LONG-TERM DISABILITY INSURANCE

Long-term disability insurance _____ lost income if you're unable to work for a long period of time due to an illness or injury.

Find a policy that covers 60–70% of your annual _____.

"People who win with money have a good *offense* **and a good** *defense.***"**

— DAVE RAMSEY

ANSWER KEY

Umbrella
Raise
Tax-free
Covers
Income

LONG-TERM CARE INSURANCE

_____-_____ care insurance covers

assisted living care, in-home care and nursing home care.

Long-term care insurance is an absolute must if you are

_____ years old or older.

IDENTITY THEFT PROTECTION

Good ID theft protection includes _____

services that assign a counselor to clean up the mess.

WILLS

Everyone 18 or older needs a _____.

NOTES

LIFE INSURANCE

Life insurance replaces income that's lost due to _____.

_____ life insurance is the only life insurance you should buy.

> **"Cash value life insurance is the** *payday lender* **of the middle class."**
>
> — DAVE RAMSEY

_____ use life insurance as an investment.

Insurance is not a Baby Step. It's part of your _____.

One-Minute TAKEAWAY

_____

_____

_____

_____

_____

_____

ANSWER KEY

Death
Term
Never
Budget

WHOLE vs. TERM
Life Insurance

Here's an example:
Joe is 30 years old and has $180 budgeted
per month to spend on life insurance.

	BAD	**BETTER**	**BEST**
	WHOLE LIFE	**20-YEAR TERM**	**20-YEAR TERM**
COVERAGE	$250,000	$250,000	$500,000
PREMIUM	$180/MO	$13/MO	$20/MO
INVESTMENTS	?	$167/MO	$160/MO
INVESTMENT VALUES			
AT AGE **50**	$24,000	$144,561	$138,501
AT AGE **70**	$65,000	$1,436,222	$1,376,019

Always buy a policy that covers 10–12
times your annual income before taxes!

BUY THE RIGHT *Coverage*

Whether you drive a nice car or a beater, you want to make sure you're covered in case life decides to hit you . . . or your car. This is not the time to go cheap on your insurance policy! Work through Luke's scenario to find out why.

ON HIS WAY TO WORK, LUKE HITS A CAR.

The driver of the other car experiences **$30,000** in injury costs and the passenger experiences **$75,000** in injury costs. Luke totals his car and the **$50,000** car of the other driver. For each of the coverage options below, determine how much Luke will have to pay *after* his insurance pays their portion.

COVERAGE OPTION #1

To save some money up front, Luke *skimps* on insurance (bad idea, Luke!) and gets the state minimum 25/50/15 liability policy.

STATE MINIMUM COVERAGE LIMITS

25K	50K	15K

25/50/15	DRIVER	PASSENGER	DRIVER'S CAR
TOTAL COST OF ACCIDENT	$ 30,000	$ 75,000	$ 50,000
25/50/15 INSURANCE PAYS	− $ 25,000	− $ 25,000	− $ 15,000
LUKE PAYS	= $ 5,000	= $ 50,000	= $ 35,000
LUKE HAS TO PAY:	$		

Maxes at $50K

And this doesn't even include the cost to replace his own car!

COVERAGE OPTION #2

Luke watched *Financial Peace University* and knows so much more about auto insurance than he did before. Then he met with a RamseyTrusted provider to learn about the best coverage option for him. Here's what he decided on:

GOOD COVERAGE LIMITS FOR LUKE

100K	300K	100K

Covers Injuries to Individuals	**Covers the Total of All Injuries to People**	**Covers Damage to Property**
The maximum amount (in thousands of dollars) **per person** that will be covered	The maximum amount (in thousands of dollars) **per accident** that will be covered	The maximum amount (in thousands of dollars) **per accident** that will be covered

Now, work the same scenario, but this time, Luke has a good **100/300/100** insurance policy.

100/300/100	DRIVER	PASSENGER	DRIVER'S CAR
TOTAL COST OF ACCIDENT	$ 30,000	$ 75,000	$ 50,000
	— Maxes at $300K —		
100/300/100 INSURANCE PAYS	− $	− $	− $
LUKE PAYS	= $	= $	= $

LUKE HAS TO PAY: $

(of course, he still has to replace his own car.)

Respond to the following question:

1. How did this Activity help you understand the importance of getting the right coverage?

DISCUSSION

Whether you're taking the class online or in person, be honest with your answers and remember to encourage one another!

 When have you let the *cost* of insurance dictate how *much* insurance you get in a certain policy? How does this lesson challenge you to think differently?

 How do you see your fully funded emergency fund fitting into your insurance plan? How can you make sure you have the right balance between the two?

 Everyone 18 or older needs a written will. Do you have a will? If not, what has been holding you back from getting one?

 Can you imagine building wealth to the point where you can self-insure? Why or why not? How have the Baby Steps moved you closer to making that a reality?

ACTION STEPS

It's time to live out what you just learned! Complete each of the Action Steps before the next lesson.

☐ **REVIEW ALL OF YOUR COVERAGE**
Take our Coverage Checkup in **Ramsey+** to see where you need to make adjustments to your insurance plan. We'll give you a prioritized list of what to add, drop or change. This includes your will! Then we'll connect you with the service providers we recommend to knock out each item on the list!

☐ **CONNECT WITH A RAMSEYTRUSTED PROVIDER**
After working through this lesson, if you already know you're missing insurance items or you're ready to get quotes for the best rates and coverage for you, then connect with one of our RamseyTrusted providers in **Ramsey+**.

☐ **TRACK YOUR TRANSACTIONS IN EVERYDOLLAR**
Are you sensing a pattern? That's right, you need to be tracking your transactions every single week. This is the best way to make sure you're spending and saving according to the budget you created.

☐ **READ "TERM LIFE INSURANCE—THE WAY TO GO" ON THE NEXT PAGE**
We're not too big on whole life insurance. In fact, we hate it. But you should get term life insurance ASAP. Read on to learn what kind of coverage you need, and get it in place today!

Term Life INSURANCE
THE WAY TO GO

Life insurance provides security, protection and peace of mind for your family should the unthinkable happen.

So, if someone depends on your income, you need life insurance. Plain and simple. And don't wait to get this done—do it today.

WHOLE LIFE *vs.* TERM LIFE INSURANCE

Your two main options for life insurance are whole life coverage and term life. But which is better? The first is a total rip-off. The second is an inexpensive, safe plan to protect your family.

1 **Whole life insurance** is more expensive and includes a "savings" plan with a terrible return. Basically, it tries to double up as an investment account and does a lousy job of it. With term life, you'll pay a fraction of the price. Then you can simply invest the difference you would have paid for whole life insurance—like Dave explained.

2 **Term life insurance** is the easiest and least expensive way to protect your family after you're gone. Simply put, here's how it works: If you (or your spouse) die at any time during this term, your beneficiaries will receive a payout from the policy.

HOW LONG DO I NEED COVERAGE?

Dave's general rule is to buy based on when your kids will be heading off to college and living on their own. Typical terms are 10, 15, 20 or 30 years.

We recommend a 15- or 20-year term.

For example, if you have a newborn in the house, then pick up a 20-year plan. If you have a 10-year-old, a 15-year plan would be a better option for you.

HOW MUCH COVERAGE DO I NEED?

If you're getting a policy through work, we can almost guarantee it's not offering you enough coverage.

Always have a policy that covers 10–12 times your annual pretax income.

Say you're making $50,000 a year. That means you need at least $500,000 in coverage. That replaces your salary for your family if something happens to you.

And one quick note: Don't forget to get term life insurance for both spouses, even if one of you stays at home with the kids. Why? Because if the stay-at-home parent was gone, replacing that childcare and home upkeep would be expensive!

Get the Right Coverage Today!

Look, this stuff isn't easy to think about. But life is precious!

And the cost of not having a plan in place for the unthinkable is much higher than the cost of term life insurance. You need to keep your loved ones protected.

Let us help!

The ideal time to buy life insurance is now—before you need it. If you're ready to take the next step, connect with one of our **RamseyTrusted providers in Ramsey+** today!

**Slow and STEADY
wins the race.**

— DAVE RAMSEY

BUILDING WEALTH

KEY POINTS

- When you follow the Baby Steps and invest 15% of your income over time, you will become a Baby Steps Millionaire!

- Lower your risk by diversifying your investments across four types of mutual funds.

- Keep it simple and never invest in things you don't understand.

GUIDE
Dave Ramsey

God gave _____ the ability to build wealth.

Baby Step 4 is to invest _____% of your household income in retirement.

The 401(k), IRA, 403(b) and 457 are tax-_____ plans.

The Roth 401(k), Roth IRA, Roth 403(b) and Roth 457 are after-tax plans and grow tax-_____.

But *remember* the LORD your God, for it is he who gives you the ability to *produce wealth.*

— DEUTERONOMY 8:18 (NIV)

NOTES

LESSON 7 //
BUILDING WEALTH

_____ beats Roth. Roth beats traditional.

_____ funds allow investors to pool their money together to invest.

Your return comes when the _____ of the fund increases.

A COUPLE IN THEIR 30s READY TO
Invest 15%

HERE'S THE SCENARIO:

$60K Household Income	$750 Per Month ($9,000/Year)	30 YEARS From Age 35–65	11% Growth Rate

	BEST ROTH 401(k) WITH MATCH	BETTER ROTH IRA	GOOD TRADITIONAL 401(k)
3% MATCH	$421,000	$0	$0
CONTRIBUTION & GROWTH	$2,103,000	$2,103,000	$2,103,000
TOTAL AT 65	**$2,524,000**	$2,103,000	**$2,103,000**
TOTAL TAXES PAID	$105,000	$0	$526,000
TOTAL NET	**$2,419,000**	**$2,103,000**	**$1,577,000**

ANSWER KEY

Match
Mutual
Value

HOW TO INVEST
15% OF YOUR INCOME

If your company offers a Roth 401(k) with a match and good mutual fund options:

- Invest the entire 15% in that plan.

If your company offers a traditional 401(k) with a match:

- Invest an amount equal to the match.

- Next, invest up to the limit in a Roth IRA.

- If you have a higher income and hit the Roth IRA limit before you've invested 15% of your income, go back to the 401(k) and finish your investing there.

NOTES

LESSON 7 //
BUILDING WEALTH

Diversification lowers _____.

Diversify across _____ types of mutual funds: growth and income, growth, aggressive growth and international.

Give portions **to seven, yes to eight, for you do not know what** *disaster* **may come upon the land.**

— ECCLESIASTES 11:2 (NIV84)

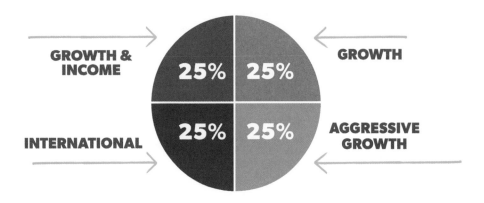

DIVERSIFY ACROSS
4 types **OF MUTUAL FUNDS**

GROWTH & INCOME — 25%
GROWTH — 25%
INTERNATIONAL — 25%
AGGRESSIVE GROWTH — 25%

ANSWER KEY

Risk
Four

Never _____ on your retirement plan.

Never _____ in something you don't understand.

Lazy hands make for poverty, but diligent hands *bring wealth.*

— **PROVERBS 10:4** (NIV)

WHAT COULD YOUR MONEY *Turn Into?*

Your most powerful wealth-building tool is your income—until your investments start earning more than you do. That's why you want to get to **Baby Step 4** as fast as you can!

Take your current monthly gross income (what you make before taxes) and calculate how much you would invest if you were on Baby Step 4 right now.

ON BABY STEP 4, I WOULD NEED TO INVEST:

$ [_____] **x** **.15** **=** [_____]

MONTHLY GROSS INCOME   15%   MONTHLY CONTRIBUTION

Before the next lesson, you'll go to **Ramsey+** to see exactly what your monthly investment could look like in **20, 30 and 40 years** at an 11% rate of return!

For now, check out the table below to get ballpark numbers.

MONTHLY CONTRIBUTION	**20** YEARS	**30** YEARS	**40** YEARS
$700	$605,946	$1,963,163	$6,020,088
$800	$692,510	$2,243,615	$6,880,101
$900	$779,074	$2,524,068	$7,740,116

Respond to the following questions:

1. What comes to mind when you see what your monthly investment could turn into?

2. How do you feel knowing that if your income increases, you'll get to invest even *more* each month?

DISCUSSION

Whether you're taking this class online or in person, be honest with your answers and remember to encourage one another!

 Are you on track or off track to reach your retirement goals? How has this lesson helped you feel more confident in your future?

 Which tax-advantaged plans are available to you today? What's the first step you're going to take to figure out where and how you need to invest?

 Building wealth is the key to creating a legacy that will outlive you. What comes to mind when you think about the kind of legacy you want to leave?

 After watching this lesson, do you believe that investing in mutual funds over a long period of time is the best way to build wealth?

ACTION STEPS

It's time to live out what you just learned! Complete each of the Action Steps before the next lesson.

☐ **SEE WHAT YOUR INVESTMENT WILL BECOME**
In the Activity, you calculated 15% of your monthly gross income that will go into retirement savings. Ready to see what that number could become in 20, 30 and 40 years? Use **Ramsey+** to find out!

☐ **IF YOU'RE IN BABY STEPS 1–3 . . .**
Focus all your energy and extra money on saving an emergency fund or paying off debt—remember, you're not investing while you're gazelle intense! But if you have any retirement investments with a former employer, connect with a SmartVestor Pro in **Ramsey+** to learn how to do a rollover.

☐ **IF YOU'RE IN BABY STEPS 4–7 . . .**
You just learned the ins and outs of investing—you want to keep your risk low and your reward high! If you're in Baby Steps 4–7, go to **Ramsey+** to connect with a SmartVestor Pro in your area and start investing the right way.

☐ **TRACK YOUR TRANSACTIONS IN EVERYDOLLAR**
You know what to do. Get your budget up to date by tracking your transactions! This is also a great time to adjust any categories you need to.

☐ **READ "WHAT'S THE DEAL WITH CRYPTOCURRENCY?" ON THE NEXT PAGE**
Investing isn't one-size-fits-all, but there are definitely some things everyone should avoid as part of their strategy. Read on for a crash course on the latest trend: cryptocurrency.

WHAT'S THE *Deal* WITH CRYPTOCURRENCY?

IT'S ALL THE RAGE, but that doesn't make cryptocurrency a good investment strategy. In fact, get-rich-quick schemes never are! Remember the story of the tortoise and the hare? When it comes to a solid wealth-building strategy, slow and steady *always* wins the race. But what exactly is cryptocurrency, and how does it work? In this Deep Dive, we'll help you get a better understanding of crypto and take a look at three of the latest harebrained digital money schemes out there.

CRYPTOCURRENCIES are digital assets people use for investing and making online purchases. You exchange real currency, like dollars, to buy "coins" or "tokens" of a certain kind of cryptocurrency.

And they're decentralized, meaning no government or bank controls how they're made, exchanged or what their value is. So, they're super unstable. On any given day, their value may swing way up, only to come plunging back down. Plus, cryptocurrencies have an unproven rate of return (aka they lack data and credibility), making them a pretty lousy long-term investment plan.

BITCOIN
WHAT ?
Started in 2009, Bitcoin is now one of the most popular cryptocurrencies. Bitcoin users exchange their digital "coins" for goods and services or trade them for cash.

RISKS ⚠

Can you say "volatile"? Like gold, bitcoins are only worth what people are willing to pay or exchange for them. So, there's no basis for a bitcoin's value—it's completely unregulated! And the lack of a consistent pricing tool is one of the major reasons we see huge swings in a bitcoin's worth. Sure, it sounds great to have your money grow by 300% in a year, but how will you feel when the bottom drops out? And based on past performance and volatility, it most likely will.

Also, there's just too much mystery here. Transactions are anonymous and the creator has an alias with no known identity. (Is it a person? A company? No one knows.)

DOGECOIN
WHAT ?
Dogecoin (pronounced "dohj-coin") is a kind of digital money that started

out in 2013 as a joke based off of a meme of a Shiba Inu dog. Oh, we're serious. You can't make this up.

RISKS ⚠

First of all, we're talking about investing your hard-earned money in something inspired by a dog meme . . . a dog meme.

Secondly, if Bitcoin is unreliable, Dogecoin is worse. It's unstable and unpredictable. At one point, Dogecoin hit $0.4252, but by the next morning, it was down 22% at $0.3248. So, a lot can change in one day—especially if investors decide to get out while the gettin's good. And yeah, Elon Musk said this was his favorite type of cryptocurrency, but he's got money to burn. Unless you do too, skip it.

NFTs
WHAT ❓

An NFT is basically a digital collector's item, and it stands for *non-fungible token*, which is one of the weirdest terms we've ever heard. So, what's it mean? Well, a dollar bill is fungible—meaning a $1 bill holds the same value as another $1 bill. It's a one-for-one trade. But if something is non-fungible, it's unique all on its own—like a baseball card, Pokémon cards or a piece of artwork. Speaking of . . . NFT art is one of the most common ways to collect NFTs.

RISKS ⚠

NFT art is digital artwork that only exists in a digital world on the *blockchain* (which is like a digital ledger where ownership is recorded). So, even though anyone can copy anything on the internet a million times over, there's only one true digital owner of it (whatever *it* is), and the NFT proves that.

Here's the craziest part: Unlike Pokémon cards or a literal piece of art, NFTs don't exist in real life! They're all digital. So, even though you pay for something, all you get to show for it is your one-of-a-kind digital token called an NFT. But hey, you have digital ownership and bragging rights (but no copyrights) to some obscure artwork on the internet! Congratulations?

IT COMES DOWN TO THIS:

If you're on Baby Step 4 and have 15% of your income invested in mutual funds with a history of strong performance *and* you want to spend some of your budgeted fun money playing with cryptocurrency—go for it. But the key word here is *playing* . . . or maybe *gambling*. Because you need to be ready and willing to lose it. Yes, some people have gotten rich with cryptocurrency. Just like some people have gotten rich at the blackjack table. That doesn't mean you should risk your retirement and your future security on a gamble.

Long story short? Don't invest in crypto. These are high-risk gambles, not sound investment strategies.

Instead, connect with a **SmartVestor Pro in Ramsey+** and start investing the right way for the long haul—slow and steady.

The grass at your house feels **DIFFERENT** when you own it.

— **DAVE RAMSEY**

BUYING & SELLING YOUR HOME

KEY POINTS

- A house is the largest financial investment you will ever make.

- Here's your home-buying plan: a 15-year fixed-rate mortgage with at least a 10% down payment and monthly payments that are no more than 25% of your take-home pay.

- When you pay off your home, you're 100% debt-free!

LESSON 8 //
BUYING & SELLING YOUR HOME

GUIDE
Dave Ramsey

BENEFITS OF HOMEOWNERSHIP

It's a steady _____ plan.

Your home grows virtually _____-_____.

The National Study of Millionaires reveals that one of the two most important milestones for the typical millionaire is that their home is paid off _____.

SAVE YOUR DOWN PAYMENT

If you get a mortgage, get a _____-year fixed-rate loan.

GET PREAPPROVED FOR A MORTGAGE

Your mortgage payments, including HOA fees, insurance and taxes, should be no more than _____% of your take-home pay.

_____ any of these mortgage options:

- Adjustable-rate mortgage (ARM)
- Interest-only mortgage
- Reverse mortgage
- Subprime mortgage
- Balloon mortgage
- United States Department of Agriculture/Rural Housing Service (USDA/RHS) mortgage
- Accelerated or biweekly payoff programs
- Any mortgage with a prepayment penalty

ANSWER KEY

Growth
Tax-free
Early
15
25
Avoid

LESSON 8 //
BUYING & SELLING YOUR HOME

Overall, a conventional loan is the _____ way to finance your home. These are typically Fannie Mae (FNMA) and are privately insured against default.

An FHA loan is backed by the Federal Housing Association and is often for first-time home buyers. It's insured by the U.S. Department of Housing and Urban Development (HUD) and is more expensive than a conventional loan.

A VA loan is backed by the Department of Veterans Affairs and allows veterans to buy a home with virtually no down payment. These loans have a high funding fee and are also more expensive than a conventional loan.

FIND A REAL ESTATE AGENT

Make sure you _____ at least three real estate agents.

ANSWER KEY

Best
Interview

NOTES

GO HOUSE HUNTING

Buy in the _____ price range of the neighborhood.

Homes appreciate in good neighborhoods and
are _____ based on three things: location,
location, location.

Buy bargains by overlooking things that can be _____,
like bad landscaping and ugly carpet or wallpaper.

Always buy a home that is or can be attractive from the street
and has a good _____ plan.

As for me and my house,
we will *serve the Lord.*

— JOSHUA 24:15 (ESV)

NOTES

LESSON 8 //
BUYING & SELLING YOUR HOME

NOTES

SUBMIT AN OFFER

You'll make an offer and make an earnest money deposit—this is 1–3% of the offer amount.

MEET CONTINGENCIES UNDER CONTRACT

When you buy property that's not a subdivision lot, always get a _____ survey.

Always have a professional home _____.

_____ insurance insures you against an unclean title when your property ownership is called into question.

CLOSE ON YOUR HOME

On average, you'll pay 3–4% of the purchase price of your home in closing fees.

SELLING YOUR HOME

Have your agent do a detailed comparative _____ analysis (CMA) to accurately price your home.

Think like a _____ and make over your home like a model home.

> **"100% of** *foreclosures* **happen on homes with a** *mortgage***."**
>
> **— DAVE RAMSEY**

HOME THE THE RIGHT WAY

Drew & Amy and Charles & Misty each put **20%** down on a **$225,000** home at a **4%** annual interest rate.

$225,000 HOME	DREW & AMY	CHARLES & MISTY

MORTGAGE (FIXED)	**30-YEAR**	**15-YEAR**
PAYMENT (MONTHLY)	**$859**	**$1,331**
TOTAL	**$309,364** AFTER 30 YEARS	**$239,658** AFTER 15 YEARS

WHILE DREW & AMY PAY LESS IN THE SHORT TERM, HOW MUCH MORE DO THEY PAY OVERALL?

$_____

(Hint: $309,364 - $239,658)

Respond to the following questions:

 1. Based on this example, would you rather be Drew & Amy or Charles & Misty? Why?

 2. Charles & Misty will save more money than Drew & Amy, and they'll pay off their home 15 years sooner! How does this make you feel about your current or future mortgage situation?

DISCUSSION

Whether you're taking the class online or in person, be honest with your answers and remember to encourage one another!

 When you picture your dream home, what do you see? What parts of your home stand out, and why are they important to you?

 Based on what you've learned from Dave, how do you know if you have too much house?

 Based on your answer to the last question, do you need to make any adjustments to your housing situation? If so, what? Refinance? Downsize? Throw more money at your mortgage?

 If you're a homeowner, think about life without a mortgage. What could you do with the extra money that's currently going toward payments? If you're renting, how do you feel about owning a home someday? How could you save up for one?

ACTION STEPS

It's time to live out what you just learned! Complete each of the Action Steps before the next lesson.

☐ **SEE HOW FAST YOU CAN PAY OFF A HOUSE**
Whether or not you're currently a homeowner, head over to **Ramsey+** to discover how quickly you could pay off a home (maybe the one you're in right now!) in Baby Step 6 by making extra payments on your mortgage.

☐ **IF YOU'RE IN BABY STEP 3B . . .**
First, discover how much house you can afford in **Ramsey+**. Then, as you save more and more toward your down payment goal, track your progress in your membership. Finally, when you're ready to buy a home, connect with a local real estate agent who is RamseyTrusted.

☐ **SCHEDULE A BUDGET COMMITTEE MEETING**
You're coming up on your next budgeting cycle, so it's time for another Budget Committee Meeting. For your next budget, pay close attention to how much you're paying toward housing each month. Do you have too much house? And don't forget to track your transactions in **EveryDollar**.

☐ **COMPLETE YOUR FINANCIAL SNAPSHOT**
If you're in a class, fill out your second Financial Snapshot card (page 129) and turn it in to your coordinator at the start of Lesson 9. Then celebrate your progress!

☐ **READ "PMI: NECESSARY OR NOT?" ON THE NEXT PAGE**
This Deep Dive shares a little more about why you should avoid private mortgage insurance and how to get rid of it once and for all.

PMI:
NECESSARY *or Not?*

We're going to save you $10,000 before this article ends. Ready?

You've worked the Baby Steps, done your research, and kept an eye on the housing market. You're ready to buy a home. If you can't put 100% down, you'll move through a mortgage approval process where you may encounter **private mortgage insurance** (PMI).

Hold on a second. You might be asking yourself, *Was this on the list of the eight insurances I need to have?* We're glad you asked. The answer is no. And here's why.

AT A GLANCE

PMI = PRIVATE MORTGAGE INSURANCE

IF YOU PUT 20% DOWN, YOU AVOID IT

RATES RANGE FROM 0.5–1.5% OF HOME LOAN AMOUNTS

WHAT IS PMI?

PMI protects the lender. You're about to borrow a lot of money, and your lender wants to make sure they get their money back if you can't make the payments and end up in foreclosure. Every year, there are between 500,000 and 1.5 million home foreclosures, so you can understand why lenders want insurance. **PMI protects their investment.**

But here's the catch: You're the one who will be paying the insurance premiums—*not* them.

HOW MUCH DOES PMI COST?

PMI rates can range anywhere from 0.5–1.5% or more of your loan amount. For this example, let's use a 1% PMI rate and a $200,000 home loan amount.

At 1%, your PMI would be $2,000 per year—that's an extra $166.67 per month added to your mortgage payment. After five years, PMI has added **$10,000** to the cost of your home. (There's that $10,000 you can save yourself.)

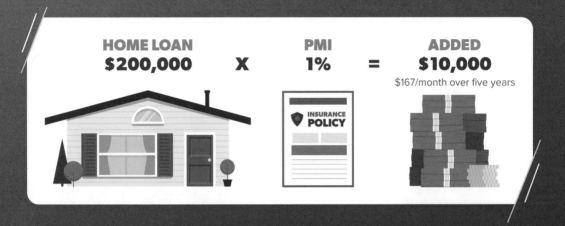

HOME LOAN		PMI		ADDED
$200,000	**X**	**1%**	**=**	**$10,000**
				$167/month over five years

HOW CAN I AVOID PMI?

The easiest way to avoid PMI is to put at least **20% down** on your home. That completely eliminates PMI. If you *don't* put 20% down, PMI will be added to your loan automatically! You won't be able to get rid of it until you've paid down your loan enough to have 20–25% equity in your home. Basically, your loan-to-value amount has to be less than 80%.

HAVE A PLAN AND USE A PROFESSIONAL

If you're going to buy a home and get a mortgage, stick to this plan: Find a real estate agent you trust and get a 15-year fixed-rate mortgage with at least 10% down (though 20% is best), and make sure the total payments (including PMI) are no more than 25% of your take-home pay.

Let us help!

Ready to find a real estate agent you trust?
Go to **Ramsey+** to find a real estate agent who is RamseyTrusted. They'll help walk you through the home-buying process.

When you LIVE like no one else, later you can live and GIVE like no one else.

— DAVE RAMSEY

In a class?

DO THIS

Be sure you're updating your savings or debt payoff progress in **Ramsey+**!

THEN DO THIS

Fill out the back of this card. Your coordinator will collect this card at the start of Lesson 9. (Do not put your name on this card.)

GENEROSITY

KEY POINTS

- If we all became outrageously generous, we could completely change the landscape of America.

- God is a giver, and because we're made in His image, we are designed to be generous!

- God owns it all. We are just managers of His money.

LESSON 9 //
OUTRAGEOUS
GENEROSITY

GUIDE
Dave Ramsey

TRUE FINANCIAL PEACE

The _____ in financial peace comes from outrageous generosity.

"**You cannot** *shake hands* **with a clenched fist.**"

— INDIRA GANDHI

GIVING CHANGES YOU

We are happiest and most fulfilled when serving and _____.

A generous person will *prosper*; whoever refreshes others will be *refreshed.*

— PROVERBS 11:25 (NIV)

GENEROSITY COULD CHANGE AMERICA

If "we the people" increased our giving a _____ percentage points, we could do things like eradicate domestic hunger, fund adoption from foster care, and build hospitals.

ANSWER KEY

Peace
Giving
Few

LESSON 9 //
OUTRAGEOUS
GENEROSITY

WHY GOD TELLS US TO GIVE

The more generous you become, the more you're becoming who God _____ you to be.

You shall truly *tithe* all the increase of your grain that the field produces *year by year.*

— DEUTERONOMY 14:22 (NKJV)

NOTES

ANSWER KEY

Made

LESSON 9 //
OUTRAGEOUS GENEROSITY

TITHES AND OFFERINGS

The tithe is a _____ of your increase.

The Bible says to give your tithe off the _____ (firstfruits).

The tithe goes to your local _____.

Offerings are above the tithe and are freely given from _____.

OWNERS AND MANAGERS

God owns it all. We are just asset _____ for the Lord.

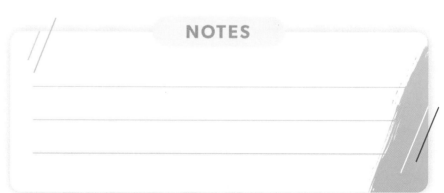

The *earth* is the LORD's, and the *fulness* thereof.

— PSALM 24:1 (KJV)

NOTES

LESSON 9 //
OUTRAGEOUS
GENEROSITY

DEBT FREEDOM

The Bible calls sin "debt," but Jesus already paid that debt. The only thing you have to do to become debt-free is accept the gift.

For God so *loved* the world that He gave His only begotten Son, that whoever *believes* in Him should not perish but have *everlasting life.*

— **JOHN 3:16** (NKJV)

Give to look more LIKE GOD

Giving changes you. We're not trying to be mushy or corny—it's a fact. You see, God is the ultimate giver. And when we give, we start to look more like Him.

1 Chronicles 29:14 (NIV) says, "Everything comes from you, and we have given you only what comes from your hand."

Everything we have comes from God. He owns it all! When He asks us to give, it's not because He needs our money. **His goal is not to reshape economics. His goal is to reshape our hearts.**

When you give your money, your time and your talents to help and love other people, it doesn't change them as much as it changes you! And God's all about changing *you*. That's what this whole journey toward financial peace is about—changing you.

Remember, the *peace* in financial peace comes from outrageous generosity!

YOU SHOULD *always* BE A GIVER

BABY STEPS 1 2 3   In Baby Steps 1–3, you might only be giving a tithe to your local church.

BABY STEPS 4 5 6   In Baby Steps 4–6, you may have a little room in your budget to start giving offerings.

BABY STEP 7   By the time you hit Baby Step 7, you're giving from your surplus with outrageous generosity!

WAYS YOU CAN START GIVING

Jot down ideas about how you can start giving your money, time and talents today—no matter which Baby Step you're on!

MONEY

Budget a tithe (10% of your income off the top) to your local church.

Give a 100% (or more!) tip at a restaurant.

TIME

Volunteer to mentor a child in your community.

Sign up to serve at a local nonprofit or ministry you're passionate about.

TALENTS

Lend your skills and volunteer to help build a home.

Put your mechanical talents to work and help fix your neighbor's car.

DISCUSSION

Whether you're taking this class online or in person, be honest with your answers and remember to encourage one another!

 1 Remember, no matter where you are in the Baby Steps, giving should be the priority in your budget! How has this lesson helped you better understand the reason this is so important?

 2 Giving is the most fun you can have with money! How have you had fun with giving in the past? What's one way you want to be outrageously generous in the future?

 3 What keeps you from giving as much as you'd like to give? How does this lesson help you work through that hang-up?

 4 Whether you have a little or a lot, God owns it all! How does His ownership of everything affect the way you think about what He's given you to manage?

ACTION STEPS

It's time to live out what you just learned! Complete each of the Action Steps below.

☐ **GRATITUDE LEADS YOU TO CONTENTMENT**
Whether you're on Baby Step 1 or 7, God has given you something to manage. Instead of chasing what's next, stop to practice **contentment** and thank God for what He's given you. In the space below, write three things you're thankful for!

1. _____

2. _____

3. _____

☐ **LOOK BACK AND THEN CHARGE AHEAD**
No matter where you are in the Baby Steps, your life should already look different than it did before you started. In the space below, list the top three things you've learned and then list your *why*—**the reason you refuse to quit**. This is why you won't give up when things get tough and why you'll live like no one else so later you can live and *give* like no one else.

1. _____

2. _____

3. _____

I will NOT give up, because_____

_____

☐ **STAY PLUGGED IN TO YOUR RAMSEY+ MEMBERSHIP**
Want to stay on track with your goals? Every week, track transactions in **EveryDollar**, use the other tools available to you, watch videos, connect with a coach, and more!

YOUR STORY BEGAN WITH ONE DECISION—
To Change

You already took the most difficult step in your journey—the first one.

You've made it to where you are right now, and you *can* get to where you want to go next! And we're here to help.

With Ramsey+, you'll build the habits you need to win with money.

YOUR RAMSEY+ MEMBERSHIP

You have full access to exclusive courses and tools, the premium version of EveryDollar, financial coaches, custom recommendations, plus benefits like free livestreams, audiobooks and more!

Attacking debt on Baby Step 2? Complete your **debt snowball** and track your payoff progress.

Need to talk through an obstacle you're facing? Reach out to one of our **financial coaches**.

Ready to take your budget to the next level? Connect your bank to EveryDollar and watch the *Budgeting That Actually Works* course.

Want a refresher on mutual funds? Rewatch a lesson and find a **SmartVestor Pro** to start investing in Baby Step 4.

When you work the plan, the plan works for you!

Go use everything available to you in your **Ramsey+ membership,** and keep your momentum moving forward.

You got this.

STAY MOTIVATED ON
Your Journey

Build wealth, strengthen your relationships, and
reach your goals with more from our Ramsey Team.

SHOWS
Subscribe to the Ramsey Network
and follow our shows on radio,
podcast and YouTube.
ramseysolutions.com/shows

EVENTS
Hear from our Ramsey Team in
person! Reserve your seat at one
of our upcoming live events.
ramseysolutions.com/events

BOOKS
Dive deeper with one (or all) of our
bestselling books about money,
mental health and work that matters.
ramseysolutions.com/store/books

Change lives AS A
FINANCIAL PEACE UNIVERSITY COORDINATOR

The two biggest reasons people become *Financial Peace University* coordinators are to stay motivated on their plan and to help others win with money! When you lead a *Financial Peace University* class, you get the opportunity to help others who are exactly where you started—people who are stressed, overwhelmed and ready to make a change.

And you don't need to be out of debt or have any special training to lead a class. If you want to share *Financial Peace University* with others, then you're the perfect person to become a coordinator!

In fact, we make it easy to lead a class on your schedule.

YOU PICK THE TIME
Classes meet once a week for each lesson—at a time that works best for you.

YOU PICK THE DATE
Classes meet year-round. We'll help you set a date that's convenient for your schedule.

YOU PICK THE PLACE
Your class can meet at a church, local community center or at your home.

Spread hope!

Visit **ramsey.link/leadfpu** to connect with someone from our team about starting and leading a class.

Spread hope to people right in your community and change lives as a *Financial Peace University* coordinator.

BUDGET FORMS & KEY TERMS

(More fun stuff!)

BUDGETING FORMS

Building new budgeting habits is a lot easier with the right tools. That's why we created **EveryDollar**—so you can easily make a plan for your money every month.

If you need a little extra guidance for budgeting weekly or budgeting for irregular income, the following forms will help you out! Read through the step-by-step instructions on these example forms, then go to **Ramsey+** to print out blank versions of these forms to fill out yourself.

Hey, Nerds!

If you love pen-and-paper planning, you can find more forms—including extra budgeting forms—in **Ramsey+**.

How to Set Up Your
Quick-Start Budget

Getting everything on paper first is super helpful. Then, we suggest downloading EveryDollar to help you keep up with your budget all month.

Pro tip: Before you start, open up your online bank account or grab your bank statements to help as you start filling out these numbers.

1 ## List your income.

In the Planned column for income, list out each paycheck (and any side hustles) coming in this month. Add that up. This is how much money you have to work with this month!

INCOME	PLANNED
Paycheck 1	$2,150
Paycheck 2	$2,150
TOTAL	$4,300

2 ## List your expenses.

Plan for everything you're spending money on this month.

You'll see lots of common budget categories and lines. Skip any you don't need. As you go, add the planned amounts inside each box.

HOUSING	PLANNED
Rent/Mortgage	
HOA Fees	
TOTAL	

FOOD	PLANNED
Groceries	$600
Restaurants	$50
	$650

TRANSPORTATION/GAS	PLANNED
TOTAL	$430

3 ## Subtract your expenses from your income.

This should equal zero. If you've got money left over, put it toward your debt or other money goals. If you've got a negative number, lower your planned totals or cut extras until you get zero.

4 ## Track your expenses (all month long).

How do you stay on top of your spending? Track. Your. Transactions. That means you're tracking everything that happens with your money all month long.

5 ## Make a new budget (before the month begins).

Your budget won't change too much from month to month, but no two months are exactly the same. So, create a new budget every single month! Don't forget month-specific expenses (like holidays or seasonal purchases).

Quick-Start Budget

INCOME	PLANNED
Paycheck 1	$
Paycheck 2	$
TOTAL	$

GIVING	PLANNED
TOTAL	$

SAVING	PLANNED
TOTAL	$

FOOD	PLANNED
Groceries	$
Restaurants	$
TOTAL	$

UTILITIES	PLANNED
Water	$
Electricity	$
TOTAL	$

HOUSING	PLANNED
Rent/Mortgage	$
HOA Fees	$
TOTAL	$

TRANSPORTATION/GAS	PLANNED
TOTAL	$

INSURANCE	PLANNED
Health	$
Auto	$
Renters	$
Term Life	$
TOTAL	$

DEBT	PLANNED
Credit Cards	$
Student Loans	$
Car Payments	$
Medical	$
TOTAL	$

FUN MONEY	PLANNED
TOTAL	$

MISCELLANEOUS	PLANNED
TOTAL	$

TOTAL INCOME $

TOTAL EXPENSES $

Your Goal Every Month:
Total Income - Total Expenses = $0

Need a blank form?

Download EveryDollar, plug in your numbers, and make budgeting way easier month to month.

DIRECTIONS FOR
Allocated Spending *Planning*

If you want to budget based on your pay period rather than the month, this form is for you!
The four columns on this form represent the four weeks in a given month. If you're married,
combine both of your incomes and then follow the steps below to allocate your spending.

❶ Fill out your pay period dates and list your income.

Your **pay period dates** are how long you go between
paychecks. (For example, if you get paid on the 1st and
15th, your pay periods for July would be 7/1 to 7/14 and
7/15 to 7/29.)

Pay Period Dates	7/1 TO 7/14
Pay Period Income	$2,500

Your **pay period income** is how much you make during that time. (So, if you take home $5,000 a
month, but half of that each pay period, your pay period income is $2,500.)

❷ List your expenses—thinking about due dates as you go.

Use your online bank account or copies of your bills to list your expenses in the Planned columns
based on when they're due.

Start with essentials, then extras. As you go, keep a
running total of how much of your income is left in the
Remaining column.

🏠 HOUSING	Planned	Remaining
Mortgage/Rent	$1,000	$1,250
Water	$50	$1,200

This is the trickiest step. Make sure you're covering the bills
that are due during each pay period and dividing up other
expenses, like groceries and gasoline, across pay periods.

❸ Plan for each category on the list until you hit zero.

Plan for each category on the list until the Remaining column hits **zero**. When that happens,
you're done budgeting for that pay period!

❹ Track your expenses (all month long).

If you've planned for every category and still have money left over in the Remaining column,
go back and adjust an area, such as savings or giving, so that you spend every single dollar.
Every dollar needs a job to do!

❺ Make a new budget (before the month begins).

And don't forget month-specific expenses (like holidays or seasonal purchases).

Allocated Spending

Pro tip: Keep an extra $100-300 in your checking account as a buffer.

Pay Period Dates	7/1 TO 7/14	7/15 TO 7/29	TO	TO
Pay Period Income	$2,500	$2,500		

♥ GIVING

Income - Church = Remaining Income to budget this pay period

	Planned	Remaining	Planned	Remaining	Planned	Remaining	Planned	Remaining
Church	$250	$2,250	$250	$2,250				
Charity								

Subtract the next Planned amount to get your next Remaining balance.

🐷 SAVINGS

	Planned	Remaining	Planned	Remaining	Planned	Remaining	Planned	Remaining
Emergency Fund								

🏠 HOUSING

	Planned	Remaining	Planned	Remaining	Planned	Remaining	Planned	Remaining
Mortgage/Rent	$1,000	$1,250						
Water	$50	$1,200						
Natural Gas			$35	$2,215				
Electricity			$100	$2,115				
Cable/Internet			$40	$2,075				
Trash								

Need a blank form?

We've provided an example form on the next couple pages to help! **To get a blank form, use the QR code.**

update QR CODE and the pdf that it points to.

| Pay Period Dates | 7/1 TO 7/14 | 7/15 TO 7/29 | TO | TO |

🚗 TRANSPORTATION

	Planned	Remaining	Planned	Remaining	Planned	Remaining	Planned	Remaining
Gas	$100	$1,100	$100	$1,975				
Maintenance								

🍴 FOOD

	Planned	Remaining	Planned	Remaining	Planned	Remaining	Planned	Remaining
Groceries	$320	$780	$320	$1,655				
Restaurants								

👕 PERSONAL

	Planned	Remaining	Planned	Remaining	Planned	Remaining	Planned	Remaining
Clothing			$100	$1,555				
Phone			$150	$1,405				
Fun Money	$30	$750	$40	$1,365				
Hair/Cosmetics	$60	$690						
Subscriptions			$10	$1,355				

☀ LIFESTYLE

	Planned	Remaining	Planned	Remaining	Planned	Remaining	Planned	Remaining
Pet Care			$40	$1,315				
Childcare								
Entertainment								
Miscellaneous	$50	$640	$150	$1,165				

Pay Period Dates	7/1 TO 7/14	7/15 TO 7/29	TO	TO

♥ HEALTH

	Planned	Remaining	Planned	Remaining	Planned	Remaining	Planned	Remaining
Gym								
Medicine/Vitamins			$50	$1,115				
Doctor Visits	$50	$590						

🏠 INSURANCE

	Planned	Remaining	Planned	Remaining	Planned	Remaining	Planned	Remaining
Health Insurance			$400	$715				
Life Insurance			$40	$675				
Auto Insurance	$90	$500						
Homeowners/Renters	$20	$480						
Identity Theft								

💳 DEBT

When Remaining equals zero, you're done budgeting for this pay period!

	Planned	Remaining	Planned	Remaining	Planned	Remaining	Planned	Remaining
Car Payment	$480	$0						
Credit Card 1			$150	$525				
Credit Card 2			$60	$465				
Credit Card 3								
Student Loan			$400	$65				
Medical Bill			$65	$0				
Personal Loan								

Irregular Income Budget Planning

If you've got an irregular income, plan low. What's the lowest irregular paycheck you've gotten in the last few months?

$ _____

Use that when planning your income. You can adjust later if you make more or less! Also, always cover needs before the extras.

You. Got. This.

① List your planned income.
In the Planned column for income, list out each paycheck coming in this month. For the irregular paychecks, go with that lowest amount you wrote above.

INCOME	PLANNED
Paycheck 1	$2,150
Paycheck 2	$2,150
TOTAL	$4,300

② List your planned expenses.
Use your online bank account or statements to plan what you're paying for this month.

You'll see lots of common budget categories and lines. Fill in only the ones you use, or rename lines if needed.

Note: You might have to skip some extras (or plan low) for now. If you make more than planned, see step 5.

HOUSING	PLANNED
Rent/Mortgage	$1,075
HOA Fees	$50
TOT	

FOOD	PLANNED
Groceries	$600
Restaurants	$50

TRANSPORTATION/GAS	PLANNED
TOTAL	$430

3 Subtract expenses from your income.

This should equal zero. If you've got money left over, put it toward your debt or other money goals. If you've got a negative number, lower your planned totals or cut extras until you get zero.

		INCOME
−	🏠	EXPENSES
=		$0

4 Track your expenses (all month long).

Track (and subtract) every expense you make in the Spent column so you don't overspend.

5 Make adjustments on payday.

When your paychecks come in, put the amount under the Actual column.

If you made more than planned, go to the Adjustments column and add that money to lines you skipped or planned low. If you make less than planned, subtract money from a nonessential line.

INCOME	PLANNED	ADJUSTMENTS ±
Paycheck 1	$2,150	$
Paycheck 2	$2,150	−$50

FOOD	PLANNED	ADJUSTMENTS ±
Groceries	$600	−$50
Restaurants	$50	$
TOTAL	$650	$600

6 Make a new budget (before the month begins).

And don't forget month-specific expenses (like holidays or seasonal purchases).

Irregular Income Budget

INCOME	PLANNED	ADJUSTMENTS ±	ACTUAL
Paycheck 1	$	$	$
Paycheck 2	$	$	$
Paycheck 3	$	$	$
Paycheck 4	$	$	$
TOTAL	$	$	$

GIVING	PLANNED	ADJUSTMENTS ±	SPENT
TOTAL	$	$	$

SAVING	PLANNED	ADJUSTMENTS ±	SPENT
TOTAL	$	$	$

FOOD	PLANNED	ADJUSTMENTS ±	SPENT
Groceries	$	$	$
Restaurants	$	$	$
TOTAL	$	$	$

UTILITIES	PLANNED	ADJUSTMENTS ±	SPENT
Water	$	$	$
Electricity	$	$	$
TOTAL	$	$	$

HOUSING	PLANNED	ADJUSTMENTS ±	SPENT
Rent/Mortgage	$	$	$
HOA Fees	$	$	$
TOTAL	$	$	$

TRANSPORTATION/GAS	PLANNED	ADJUSTMENTS ±	SPENT
TOTAL	$	$	$

INSURANCE	PLANNED	ADJUSTMENTS ±	SPENT
Health	$	$	$
Auto	$	$	$
Homeowners/Renters	$	$	$
Term Life	$	$	$
TOTAL	$	$	$

DEBT	PLANNED	ADJUSTMENTS ±	SPENT
Credit Cards	$	$	$
Student Loans	$	$	$
Car Payments	$	$	$
Medical	$	$	$
TOTAL	$	$	$

FUN MONEY	PLANNED	ADJUSTMENTS ±	SPENT
TOTAL	$	$	$

MISCELLANEOUS	PLANNED	ADJUSTMENTS ±	SPENT
TOTAL	$	$	$

What's Next?

Download EveryDollar, plug in your numbers, and make budgeting way easier month to month.

TOTAL INCOME: $

TOTAL EXPENSES: $

Your Goal Every Month:
Total Income - Total Expenses = $0

Key Terms

Money shouldn't be complicated. **We make it simple.** Here's a breakdown of the words and phrases used in the last nine lessons in a way that's easy to understand.

SAVING & BUDGETING

Baby Steps: Dave Ramsey's proven seven-step path for winning with money.

Budget: A monthly plan, either on paper or digital, that puts every dollar you make into a specific category.

Four Walls: The most basic expenses you need to cover to keep your family going: your food, your utilities, your shelter and your transportation.

Money Market Mutual Fund: Basically, a savings account you can open with a mutual fund company instead of a bank; it usually earns a little more interest than a bank savings account thanks to short-term mutual fund investments.

Sinking Fund: Setting aside money over time so you can buy something with cash—for example, saving $400 a month for 10 months to buy a $4,000 car.

Zero-Based Budget: A monthly budget that puts every dollar you earn into specific categories—so when your income is subtracted from your expenses, you come up with zero.

DEBT

Annual Percentage Rate (APR): The amount that borrowed money costs you each year; the APR includes your interest rate and other related fees you have to pay on a loan.

Debt Snowball: A list of all debts (except your house) from smallest to largest. You'll make minimum payments on all of them while you attack the smallest debt with a vengeance. Once that debt is gone, take that payment and apply it to the second-smallest debt. Keep this going until you've paid off the last, largest debt.

FICO Score: A number used to evaluate your "credit worthiness"; it's really an "I love debt" score that's based on your debt history, how much debt you currently have, how long you've been in debt, new debt, and the kind of debt you have.

Interest Rate: An extra percentage you pay to a lender for money you borrow.

Introductory Rate: A marketing tool that offers a lower-than-normal interest rate during the early stages of a loan; it's a rate designed to attract new customers, and it almost always goes up over time.

Navient: A student loan service that split off from Sallie Mae in 2013.

Sallie Mae: Originally a government program known as the Student Loan Marketing Association (SLMA), it's still the largest private student loan lender in the country.

SPENDING

Brand Recognition: A marketing term that measures just how aware customers are of particular brands.

Buyer's Remorse: Feeling of doubt or regret about a purchase soon after making it.

Financing: Using debt to buy something; it can also refer to the attractive terms and conditions companies use to market what they want you to buy with debt.

Impulse Purchase: Buying something without thinking about the bigger picture.

INSURANCE

Cash Value Life Insurance: Basically, a permanent life insurance policy (as opposed to a term policy) that charges high premiums and puts money in a savings account with low return rates; also referred to as whole life, universal life and variable life. Never buy this kind of life insurance.

Claim: The paperwork you send to an insurance company when you want them to cover a loss.

Coverage: The amount of protection you get from an insurance company when you suffer a loss.

Deductible: The money you pay out of pocket before insurance benefits kick in.

Health Savings Account (HSA): A tax-free savings account that sets aside money for medical expenses.

Liability: The amount of your financial obligation when you're found at fault in an accident.

Policy: In insurance, a contract that explains what is covered and what is not.

Premium: The regular payment you make to an insurance company to ensure coverage; it can be a monthly, quarterly or annual payment.

Stop Loss: For insurance, the maximum amount of out-of-pocket expenses you pay each year.

Term Life Insurance: Life insurance that remains in force for a certain period (a term); if someone depends on your income, you need term life insurance.

INVESTING

401(k): A retirement savings plan through a business where employees set aside tax-deferred income from each paycheck.

401(k) Match: A company benefit where an employer "matches" a percentage of what an employee sets aside for retirement.

403(b): A tax-favored retirement plan for public school and nonprofit employees.

Compound Interest: Interest that gets paid on both the money you put in (your principal) and on the interest you've already earned.

Direct Transfer: Moving the money from one tax-deferred retirement plan into another approved plan; because none of the money goes to you, there are no immediate tax liabilities or penalties. Also known as a *rollover*. Often used when moving from one company to another.

Diversification: Spreading money across different kinds of investments to minimize risk.

Individual Retirement Arrangement (IRA): A tax-deferred plan where workers can save some of their income for retirement; as the plan's value grows, the money isn't taxed until it's taken out.

Liquidity: A measure of how easy it is to get to your money from an account; the easier the access, the more liquid it is.

Mutual Fund: An investing tool where a group of people combine their money to create a fund of several different stocks.

Risk: The level of uncertainty about the potential returns on an investment.

Rollover: See Direct Transfer.

Roth 401(k): An employer-sponsored retirement plan funded with after-tax money; since taxes have already been paid, the account grows tax-free.

Roth IRA: A personal retirement account that grows tax-free because it's funded with after-tax dollars.

Share: How much an individual investor owns in a publicly traded company.

MORTGAGE

Adjustable-Rate Mortgage (ARM): A mortgage where the interest rate changes—usually going up—periodically; this allows banks to transfer risk to consumers through higher interest rates.

Comparative Market Analysis (CMA): The estimated value of property based on what similar properties in the area have sold for.

Curb Appeal: How nice a house looks to someone passing by.

Equity: How much of your property you own compared to how much you still owe on it; usually seen in terms of how much of a mortgage amount you've actually paid.

Fannie Mae (FNMA): The Federal National Mortgage Association; a privately owned company that deals in mortgages.

Fixed Rate: An interest rate that never changes over time; considered a much better option than an adjustable rate.

Inflation Hedge: An asset that increases in value over time and counters a rising inflation rate.

Mortgage: A loan arrangement made for buying real estate; the property serves as collateral for the loan.

Multiple Listing Service (MLS): A computer program used by real estate agents to search updated property listings.

Principal: For investments, the original amount of money put in the investment; for loans, the actual payoff amount of a loan, not including interest or other fees.

Private Mortgage Insurance (PMI): Insurance that protects a lender from a borrower who defaults on a mortgage; usually required when the borrower has paid less than 20% of the mortgage value.

GIVING

Firstfruits: The first produce gathered during a harvest, typically given as an offering to God in the Bible.

Great Misunderstanding: The mistaken belief that you get more by holding tightly to what you have instead of keeping an open hand.

Offering: A gift given above and beyond the tithe; freewill gifts given without a sense of obligation or expectation.

Stewardship: The act of managing the resources God has given each of us for His glory.

Tithe: A gift of the first 10% of one's income given to the local church.

"

There is ultimately only one **way to** *FINANCIAL PEACE,* and that is to **walk daily with** the *PRINCE OF PEACE,* **CHRIST JESUS.**

"

— DAVE RAMSEY

$27,275.97 in 7 mnths 5 days!
Andrea and Joshua Hahn
We did this for you Maverick!
Thanks, Dave!

We are debt free!
$123,495
Ron & Colleen Barger
THANK YOU DAVE!!!

$249 k in 4 yrs!
Andrew, Kelly, AJ Weisner
Columbus, Indiana

We're DEBT FREE!!
191,300.00 in 10 months
We SOLD our Rental ☺
Thank-you Lord!!
Jesse ♡ Carol

Nate, Laura, Nathan,
Luke, and Rachel
McDonell
$96,000 in 37
months!!!
"We're Debt Free!"

Ben & Alyson Baxter
$80,000 in 36 months

Jarrod & Stefanie Staggs
122k in 36 months!!
DEBT FREE!!! WOOOO!

Andy From Inwood, WV
$206,000 in 44 months
Love the Financial Peace

FREEDOM!!!
Living like no
one else so
later we can
live like no
one else!
22k/18 mos
Cash flowing
20K for school!!
Sebastian &
Mackenzie
Sanchez